Emergency Rations
What's so important we can't leave it at home?

#EdTechRations

Edited by David Hopkins

DAVID HOPKINS

For Sarah, Joel, and Silas. And Muppet (the cat). My loving family. Thank you.

DAVID HOPKINS

Foreword by Joyce Seitzinger

As is common these days, David Hopkins is one of those friends of mine that I've never talked to. I've never heard his voice and may even struggle to recognise him straightaway if I was meeting him at the pub for a beer. But I do know that if (no, when) we do meet for that beer we will have the best conversation and immediately be on the same wavelength. You see, we've been part of that rich, generous and sharing community that is the Twitter #EdTech community since 2008. That is 9 years. A long time to all hang out together. Actually, we do more than just hang out. We support each other. We answer each other's questions. We learn with and from each other every day. And David's writing on Twitter, on his blog and in his previous books - 'What is a Learning Technologist?' and 'The Really Useful #EdTechBook' - has been among the most open, helpful and generous.

No wonder then that when David put out the call for this book, so many of us volunteered in kind. EdTechs (e-learning specialists, learning designers, learning advisors or whatever title we have) often come from very different backgrounds. Some have been teachers but not all. Most of us have developed our craft as the field has evolved and as it continues to grow. So, the opportunity to pick up tricks of the trade, sneaky shortcuts or a gadget which you've never heard of, but which becomes a non-negotiable must-have one second after hearing about it, is not to be sniffed at. David asked "What is the technology you find yourself turning around and going home for if you forget it? What can't you leave at home or work, what do you feel naked without? (in your bag, in your pocket, wearable, etc.)?" I'm not sure even he expected such a variety of answers.

Jackie Carter loves her iPhone. Sarah Honeychurch has a serious handbag. Steve Wheeler, of course cannot, be without Blogger. Alec Couros is still digging his Digg Reader. Helen Blunden needs her glasses...so she can do VR properly. And Martin Hawksey demands a watch that is like him, smart.

This book is a quintessential artefact of our #EdTech community - crowdsourced, international, humorous, full of character and oh so very, very helpful. So even though we are never far away online, now you can think of us as sitting in your office on your bookshelf or inside your eReader.

Yep. You're picturing us there now, aren't you?

Joyce Seitzinger
Director and Lead Learning Designer, Academic Tribe
Melbourne, 2017

Reviews for #EdTechRations

Rachel Challen (@RKChallen). Head of the LTSU, School of Arts & Humanities, Nottingham Trent University, UK:

> "This is a fabulous book – full of fascinating stories and images of the technology that heroes of the Educational Technology world hold dear to their hearts. The chapters show why the authors use what they use and the obvious deep connection with their 'self'. If you have ever suspected that technology has the power to add to a way of being, then this book well and truly confirms it. Technology for communication, to take and curate notes and even technology to help you not lose the technology can all be found here. I've certainly found synergies with my own 'emergency rations', some surprises, and definitely some items to go on my own shopping list! There is something for everyone in this book – enjoy."

Teresa MacKinnon(@WarwickLanguage). Principal Teaching Fellow (e-learning), School of Modern Languages and Cultures, University of Warwick, UK:

> "Reviewing this book was like listening to the personal voices of many friends, most of whom I have met through the #EdTech community. Of course, they cannot live without certain technologies, apps and websites - that much was to be expected. What delighted me was the variety of approaches to their contributions, reflecting the different individuals within this connected community. The pragmatists who admit to relying on sensible shoes and stationery, the competitive types with their heart monitors and cycling accessories, the fashion victims, the style gurus, the lovers, the makers, the artists and poets...all have one thing in common. They thrive in the connections that come with the open web. This collection reveals that if you have a PLN you are unlikely to struggle in an emergency!"

Debbie Baff (@debbaff). Senior Academic Developer, Swansea University, UK:

> "What a great idea for a book. Packed full of hidden gems and sneaky peeks into people's purses, bags and pockets. Not only does this highlight some brilliant uses for technology, each chapter also gives a really good flavour of the person behind the technology. I found that I related to the various reasoning and logic for inclusion of stuff in people's #EdTech ration lists. I was familiar with a lot of the gadgets and bits of tech but was also inspired to try some new stuff out. Maybe some of these new things (new to me at least) will be going on my list of #EdTechRations! What I really liked as well was that you don't lose sight

of the human element amongst all of this technology and that for me is really important. Packed with fab information and helpful tips about the devices, software and various bits of technological kit (both digital and analogue) that people love to take with them, this book is an absolute pleasure to read. It's funny, inspiring and informative and is definitely going to be added to my #EdTEchRations of books that I can't live without (see what I did there?). "

Derek Moore (@weblearning), Educational Technology Consultant, Weblearning, South Africa:

"It's been 10 years since my first Tweet. Since then I've met and followed dedicated and talented Ed Techies from all over the world. I've read musings on Blogger or WordPress, appreciated stunning Flickr and Instagram pics, subscribed to podcasts, laughed at their humour... but strangely never given a thought to the gear required by these prolific peeps as they #workaloud. The #EdTechRations book rectifies this production gap. David [Hopkins] has compiled an interesting backstory to all the kit and gear required to share their online activities. Some have reflected philosophically on how their gear both empowers & enslaves or explored how digital technologies contribute to their capacity. Others have illustrated what rations they have stuffed into their backpacks. Many are surprisingly cautious about new and shiny tech toys. Most have an IOS device. For those who've found and followed members of this tribe and retweeted, liked and shared their social publications and profiles, #EdTechRations gives a fascinating insight to the essential tech behind these Ed Techies."

#EdTechRations Contributors

@jsecker	Jane Secker	74
@emmsking	Emma King	77
@nickotdV	Nick Overton	79
@julianstodd	Julian Stodd	81
@S_J_Lancaster	Simon Lancaster	85
@EricStoller	Eric Stoller	87
@BryanMMathers	Bryan M Mathers	90
@milenabobeva	Milena Bobeva	91
@alexgspiers	Alex Spiers	95
@steve_collis	Steve Collis	99
@jennifermjones	Jennifer M Jones	101
@nrparmar	Nitin Parmar	104
@Darcy1968	Darcy Moore	107
@mhawksey	Martin Hawksey	109
@mattlingard	Matt Lingard	112
@ryantracey	Ryan Tracey	114
@JaneBozarth	Jane Bozarth	116
@sarahknight	Sarah Knight	118
@lindacq	Linda Castañeda	122
@RealGeoffBarton	Geoff Barton	126
@stipton	Shannon Tipton	129
	Thank you	132

What Are your 'Emergency Rations'?

Consider this ... have you ever walked out the door to go to work, the shops, the gym, etc. and realised you'd forgotten to pick up your smartphone? And then turned around and gone right back for it. Have you ever made yourself late for work, for an appointment, for a friend?

Ever got half-way to work and panicked about how you'd survive the day without this piece of plastic or metal you rely on so heavily (your smartphone, tablet, USB stick, Moleskine notebook, powerbar charger, etc.)? Do you have a device you don't mind being without, for a short time, but others you just can't bear to be apart from?

This is what I mean by 'emergency rations' - the stuff you have with you in your life (personal and/or professional) that you would make the effort to go back and get if you'd forgotten it.

What kit do we carry around with us? As teachers, academics, Learning Technologists, Instructional Designers, managers, administrators, thought leaders, change-agents, etc.? What eventualities do we perceive are going to come our way? As our lives get more digital and our devices get more diverse and hungry for power, we need to stay connected, topped-up, plugged in or just simply want to prepare for that day when faced with our audience, reminding you that you forgot to ask, "I'll be presenting from my tablet ... is that OK?"

Perhaps this tweet, from Bill Thompson[1] best sums it up:

Bill Thompson @billt · Sep 12

Have realised that I very rarely check my phone. I am however umbilically attached to my networked pocket computer, used for many tasks.

What you hold in your hand here (in paperback, PDF download or loaded to your Kindle) is a collection of different perspectives from people I admire and trust. These are people I've met on Twitter, traded tweets, shared each other's blog posts and opinions, answered questions, helped each other, collaborated on projects, written articles and books with, and generally become good friends with. Many I've also had the good fortune to meet in person and bonded with at various *#EdTech* events or conferences.

These are a small but very well formed selection of people I believe you should

---

[1] Bill Thompson @billt [9:29 AM - 12 Sep 2016].
https://twitter.com/billt/status/775249915115102209

take notice of. They have something worth listening to. This is the reason they're here, and why you're here reading this book. If you know some or all the people already then you know them and their work. What you have here is not more of their normal tweets or typical blog posts. Here is their 'behind the scene' look at the devices, tools, apps, etc. they find that they really can't do without. Here are stories or experiences or preferences that you find familiar or reflect your own outlook on forgetting your phone.

Between us we share an online network, our personal learning network (PLN), from all corners of the world and all types of education - from schools, colleges, universities as well as consultants, librarians and workplace learning leaders. There is no finer collection of educator 'leaders' in a single volume, all here telling you what, and why, they have the kit they have, and why it's important.

The way each one of the contributors has interpreted the question "what is the technology you find yourself turning around and going home for if you forget it" shows a little about the way they approach their work and their digital lives. I find myself becoming increasingly conscious of my online presence. Is this a good thing, have I become self-aware?

And that's the reason for this book. I like to learn, I want to learn, and these are the people I've learned from (and with) over the years I've been blogging and on Twitter.

The contributions here are not ordered in perhaps the way you'd think of them to be: it has been a conscious effort to *not* order them according to geographic locations (UK, US, Australia, etc.) nor group them according to style or imagery, or as 'thought pieces' versus 'device lists' versus 'reflections'. I want you to read them and take each on their own merit, and these kinds of 'logical' ordering would mean you may, unfairly, compare them to others. Each of the forty two contributions is unique in its own right, and deserves to be read, digested, reflected on and responded to in this manner too.

My hope here is that there are also a few people you've not heard of before, as well as rations they talk about you may not know, or not realised you might benefit from in your own 'ration bag'. One of my aims for the book is also to widen the way in which we think about our work - these days there really isn't any reason we shouldn't be connected and connecting around the world. We may have different time zones and different politics, but we are all learning. We are all trying to help others learn. Perhaps we can learn together. Perhaps these connections we make will be enough to spark something in someone, somewhere, that will be enough to ignite the passion for learning something new. Wouldn't that be amazing? These people here in the book, and you out there, reading it, are this already, just by being here.

What can you do?

My only regret is that there are some people I really wanted here with us but, for many different reasons, couldn't join us. There are also many more who should be here but, obviously, there just wasn't room for 'everyone'!!

The other aspect of the book is that, well, it's static and won't grow unless we work on a second or third edition. I don't know where this can go, but I guess it's a possibility.

In the meantime, why not join the likes of Steve Wheeler, Sue Beckingham, Kevin Corbett, José Picardo, Helen Blunden, Darcy Moore, Alec Couros, Stephen Heppell, Jennifer Jones, Jane Secker, etc. by writing your own 'emergency ration' blog post? Then share it. Below is the text I sent to everyone here in the book, in some form or another, as a guide for what I was looking for ... take it and make it yours! As you can see from Bryan Mathers, Linda Castañeda, James Clay and Amy Burvall, they decided to draw as well as write, and what a fantastic and colourful way to introduce us to their 'emergency rations'!

What's the Challenge?

"What is the technology you find yourself turning around and going home for if you forget it. What can't leave at home or work, what do you feel naked without? (in your bag, in your pocket, wearable, etc.)? What connects your personal and professional lives to the extent you need to alter your plans to return home or the office to 'rescue'? It would be fantastic to hear your experiences and thoughts on this (between 800-1200 words)."

Look back to the first few sentences where I introduce the book and its purpose. This is what you can write and publish. What are your 'emergency rations'? What do you have that you feel 'naked' or 'vulnerable' if you leave at home? The flip side is this though - what do you have that you wish you could leave behind, but can't?

Once you written, drawn or videoed it, then please share it! Share with those you work with. Share with those you connect and collaborate with. Share on Twitter, Share on Facebook. Share on LinkedIn, Medium, your blog, etc. Share with me ... sent me a tweet (@hopkinsdavid), use the #EdTechRations hashtag and tell me what you have and why.

@stephenheppell   **Stephen Heppell**

Trying to mend the world with learning. UK

This is a very difficult question to ponder. I sail a lovely old 1907 Oyster smack[2]; it sails pretty well - quickly enough to scare us, yet evolved enough to protect us. I drive a 1931 car which is just about useable on today's manic roads, even if a motorway outing would be a little daunting. But it is salutary to consider the technology changes across their fairly short lifetimes: when our smack, the My Alice, was built in Brightlingsea, England, the roads saw almost exclusively horses or pedestrians. That was only 110 years ago (showing her photo to a group of primary age children last year they asked, politely, if I had purchased her new!). Boats had sails not engines and fishing was a hard business that killed many, as our local churchyard testifies. A decade earlier, in 1897, H.G. Wells serialised The War of the Worlds and the surprise for today's reader is that, when the Martian's landed and started vaporising all and sundry in Surrey, it took a long time for the news to travel all the way to London! No phones, TV, not even national radio (the BBC didn't arrive until 1922). Communication was slow, local and limited. As a schoolboy in the 1960s I remember the excitement of finally seeing "live" television - via the Telstar satellite from America - and then directly from the first Moon landing. Events were happening a very long way away, and we were watching as they happened.

So, a huge change during the lifetimes of my car, my boat and indeed myself, has been simply the ability to move people and information quickly and efficiently. We take so much of this for granted now, but I remember once that my essential daily survival kit included a bag of complex connectors to allow we to patch my modem (to modulate and then demodulate my computer's signal so that it would work across the telephone network!) and I spent a LOT of time under hotel beds with a torch and crocodile clips just to get connected to the world so that I could work.

Today that connected ability lives in my hand, my pocket and my bag. It is unimaginably indispensable and reliable; I can chat to and watch my grandchildren at mealtimes from anywhere across the planet, I can follow the skippers racing single handed live across the vastness of the Southern Ocean in their Vendée Globe yachts[3], I can stream movies in preparation for my annual BAFTA Awards voting at any time, in any place. I see the huge value of all this, because I have watched it grow around all of us. Showing the very first picture messaging phones to a group of children who had not been able to develop language and I vividly remember their excitement at messaging that was for them too! Or the excitement of a group of deputy head teachers as they typed their "electronic mail" on one terminal and watched it appear, printed, magically, from another on the other side of the room! Amazing!! The pace of this is rapid.

---

[2] 1907 Oyster Smack 'My Alice': *http://www.heppell.net/sail/*

[3] Vendée Globe: *http://www.vendeeglobe.org/en/*

We face only the certainty of uncertainty.

The "mobile" phone, as it was called once it became wireless and had a handle, might be at the heart of my communication and information needs today, but the device itself is constantly morphing into something new and fresh. Yesterday's rubber-keyed Nokia plain old telephone morphed into the smart iPhone of Apple and then others. That device is now morphing into a complex data capture tool at the heart of our health and economic activity, as well as our communications. Importantly, key functions once an essential part of my day to day survival, the modem, the huge storage devices, the ability to read and write to storage media and so on, have all disappeared from my pocket or my bag. Now I just have connectivity, and an ever-present 'cloud'. Maybe that connected pocketable smart device is now my single indispensable survival tool?

Maybe, but the trouble with choosing my essential stuff today, is that it is too easy to be influenced by the importance of yesterday's discoveries. I can recall a time when I didn't have ubiquitous communication and thus I value it today. But if I think instead about the big picture - never mind the device, what capabilities do I need always and will value even more into the future, then we arrive at another answer. Reflecting, "essential" falls into two core capabilities that I need from my indispensable stuff. In broad terms, I need smallness and I need connected intelligence.

Let me explain why: back in the 1980s we did lots of work on artificial intelligence. The languages we used were clunky - Lisp, Prolog, Smalltalk - and I mainly remember inputting amazing numbers of nested brackets! The potential of AI was clear, even then, especially perhaps with rule based systems like claiming benefits, grammar, or driving a car. The computers required were vast; you needed to come to them, but quickly folk could see that by adding a bit of Moore's Law[4] and some time, the intelligence could go with you. By 1987 Apple had a clear description of their Knowledge Navigator AI agent (they made a compelling little video of it in use - watch it[5]) and that of course grew up, after a bit more of Moore's Law and further time, to be Siri in your phone, Apple TV and so on (other brands are available!). That intelligence in your navigation maps, in your online shopping, in your social communities, in the preservation of your health, in your transport is growing to be the thing you can't be without. Sailing our old Oyster smack, the once essential skills of navigating by a sextant were rapidly overhauled by GPS, but now the combination of smart navigation with real time information and complex algorithms exploring wind and weather patterns mean a whole new level of safety, and of competitive speed, when we are afloat. And all that power isn't in a vast console, it is in the pockets of everyone aboard. It's not the device that is essential, it is the intelligence to process complex real time and historical data that I can't now be safely without.

Of course, in that context, smallness matters too. Back in the 1990s I was lucky

---

[4] Moore's Law: *http://www.investopedia.com/terms/m/mooreslaw.asp*

[5] Knowledge Navigator (1987) Apple Computer: *https://youtu.be/hb4AzF6wEoc*

enough to race with Larry Ellison of his über-expensive America's Cup yacht (we'd done some neat work on early online social communities with his Oracle software). We beat our South African opponent's boat convincingly. At the end of the race a fast launch came over to us and whisked away a large memory storage device (there was too much data for a wireless connection in those days) to get it back to dock for analysis before we arrived home. In the bilge of the boat was a mini-computer the size of a small fridge. The scale, the expense, and the magnitude of the data capture meant it was only for billionaires then. Today dear old Moore's law has brought us the ability to exceed the data capture of that expensive yacht with myriad cheap connected devices: pocketable, wearable, implantable even. The Internet of Things (IoT), plus the Very Big Data that the "things" generate, with analytical intelligence added to the mix, have meant that my essential choices come down to just those two things: I want intelligent algorithms in my pocket and I want connected devices all over the place to collect the information I need. I need this now as my "emergency rations" and I will need them even more going forwards.

Never mind the actual devices involved, I need these capabilities.

@Bali_Maha   Maha Bali

Assoc Prof Prac @CLTAUC. Part of @HybridPed + @vconnecting + @DigPedLab + @ProfHacker + @dmlresearchhub. Cairo, Egypt.

I tried really hard not to choose my smartphone as my *#EdTechRation*. I even considered saying my ration is my phone's charger because, really, the day I forget that is almost as bad as leaving without the phone. I use my phone so much throughout my day, and 3G/4G connection drains the battery (because I also don't like buying a new phone every month, so it's not a brand new one these days) it should be the charger.

But I realised that even though many people are glued to their phones, not everyone uses their phone the same way. Aside from the necessity of having the phone calling and text messaging functions in case my family needs me, or email in case work needs me (I still haven't decided they don't have that right to ask for it 24/7) ... I use my phone for almost everything. I have always had an Android phone, but I also have two iPads, so I guess I am OS agnostic.

I Write
I write, boy do I write, on my phone. I blog from my phone's WordPress app. Over 90% of my blogposts have been written using that app, either in the car during my daily commute to work, or in bed. I work on Google docs. I collaborate in Google docs too, ones that result in peer-reviewed articles and grant applications. I write those mainly on Google docs on my phone: the comments appear completely different on the app than on a computer, but I am conscious of these differences and how they influence how I collaborate.

I also write all kinds of notes on my phone too. It started even before smartphones, while working on my PhD, I would need to write notes to capture thoughts at inappropriate moments, like at 3AM while feeding my baby. That practice eventually evolved to blogging from my phone, and then the Google docs and collaboration just evolved from there.

I Consume
I read on my phone. I used to travel with 4 or 5 books and several printouts of articles in my hand luggage. Now I have hundreds of books and articles on my Kindle and other phone apps. I am a very moody reader and, in the midst of reading a novel, I can decide if I want to swap and read something non-fiction or a magazine instead. With my phone, I just switch smoothly. I also annotate articles on my phone using Hypothes.is[6], or using Kindle's highlight/note options or Medium's app if it's a post on Medium. I read and comment on my students' blogs on my phone.

I listen to music and audiobooks and podcasts on my phone, especially when I

---

[6] Annotate with anyone, anywhere - *https://hypothes.is/*

am multitasking like cooking or exercising or just walking.

I Connect

The most important function of my phone is connecting, of course. Beyond phone calls and text messages, I use Twitter mainly from my phone and I have 8 accounts logged in at a time. I use Slack to communicate with teams privately, and I have 15 teams currently installed on my phone, but only about 5 of them are active in ways that require my attention. I have built some strong relationships with people via Twitter DM and built community on Slack and Facebook groups.

I also use Skype, Viber[7], Google Hangouts for video calls on my phone to connect with family and friends. I always tell people who have audio/mic problems, when using Google hangouts on their computer, to switch to phone: the phone app never has audio/mic problems. It's a phone! That's its basic function. My daughter who is only five and a half already knows what functionalities of Google hangouts work only on the computer and don't work on the phone app!

And I do a little bit of spiritual connecting through my phone as well. I read Quran on my phone. There are all these different apps for reading Quran. And I am part of this awesome WhatsApp group of women and each week we divide the chapters of the Quran amongst ourselves and we read them separately then report that we are done reading...so that, over 2 weeks, we have read all of it amongst ourselves. It's a cool digital version of the I practice of getting together in someone's house to read Quran. I bet you didn't see that one coming :)

Empower and Enslave Me

My smartphone empowers and enslaves me. As a mom, it is easier to take care of my child while handling some small tasks on my phone. I have some of her books on my Kindle app (she calls them "not real books" but she will read them). She is also young enough to tolerate book samples that don't finish the story, as long as we have a good stock of "real" books she can read. My smartphone allows me to have a social life when I can't go out at night. And it allows me to read in bed, as long as I want.

My phone also enslaves me. I am always on and always connected. But honestly, I would not have it any other way. And if I want it another way, I know how to turn on airplane mode :) so I can read on my Kindle uninterrupted.

So, my #EdTechRation is my phone. But it's really so many dimensions of my life: reading, writing, communicating. And my phone isn't your phone, because different people have different relationships with their phones.

---

[7] Viber - http://www.viber.com/

@timbuckteeth   Steve Wheeler

Teacher educator, FRSA, author, researcher, international speaker, associate professor, edupunk, open educator. Plymouth, UK

I have been asked to write a section for this book on emergency rations. I interpret this as a question: 'What are the most important elements of your tool kit that are indispensable, that you would choose to have with you, when the gates of Hell have been opened and Satan's hordes are beating down your door?' Well, in the event of The Apocalypse, most of us won't be worrying too much about what social media we have available – we'll be running for the hills. The end of the world will not be televised, or if it is, no-one will be that interested in watching.

But in terms of social media and learning, what DOES happen when everything goes south? What happens when there is a crisis and our usual access to supplies is gone? If all the shops are closed, or there is nothing on the supermarket shelves, we rely on what we have stashed away - our emergency supplies. It's then that we call on our ingenuity to survive and cope with the crisis, but it requires some forethought and planning. It's the same with our technology tool kit. Each of us has a favourite set of tools we on which we predominantly rely. But there is a deeper dimension that the mere utility of the tool.

Often, we survive best when we have others around us we can trust and confide in. And that is the clue to the most important ration of all. You see, we humans are inherently social. Our deepest desire is to be accepted by others, to feel we belong, to have someone to share our stories and to spend time with, to have someone we care about.

Social is also a key dimension in learning.

Most of our learning is achieved within social contexts. I can't think of any examples where I have learnt something significant and long lasting, without the presence of others, or at least their social influence. From language acquisition, to basic numeracy and literacy skills, to more sophisticated activities such as public speaking, dining out with old friends or driving in traffic - all have been scaffolded and coached through the influence of others. Conversations are some of the richest learning experiences, even in our senior years. Discussions prompt us to consider alternative perspectives which widen our understanding.

It follows that the most important thing we need in our technology emergency supply in a time of crisis, is the means to connect with others, and to access information and services other have provided, when we need it.

The mobile phone, it seems, has been with us forever. But it's a relatively new invention, designed and developed for personal use in the last few decades.

Originally designed as a phone, it has rapidly evolved into a device that can send text, take pictures, record video, navigate us around unfamiliar environments, and connect via the Internet to a vast array of content – and people. Now it's a smartphone, with features that include apps (applications) that include the ability to give your phone verbal instruction, enquire about just about anything, measure your calorie consumption and step count, and even....

So, to repel the Four Horsemen of the Apocalypse, here are the four key apps that make up my personal emergency rations:

Twitter: This started life as a microblogging tool, limiting users to 140 characters they could use to message those who 'followed them' (subscribed to their feed). A user's own timeline consisted of those they followed in turn, and within this simple network configuration, many rich and diverse conversations have ensued since the inception of Twitter. Twitter quickly evolved into a large global network of users, and as it became more popular it introduced many new features, including the capability to send images and multimedia files, and a private messaging service (DM or direct messaging) that has recently expanded beyond 140 characters, so that users can have protracted private conversations. I have received better continuing professional development on Twitter than through any formal education processes. Just about every day I learn something important by following links shared by my Twitter network, or through conversations. Also, I don't have to work too hard to discover content I will find useful – I simply let my Twitter network filter it and present it to me. The power of using Twitter resides in who you follow – so follow well, and remember – you are what you tweet!

Facebook: Used largely to communicate with my family and friends, but can also be used for learning – there are many Facebook pages dedicated to user groups, research communities and for learning just about anything you wish to learn. When I'm out of the country, and texting and phone calls are not possible, I almost always resort to using Facebook's private messenger tool to connect with my wife and family. Facebook is also useful for sharing photos and videos, and it is gratifying when others 'like' and comment on your status updates, because this is where social connection occurs and where rich conversations can be enjoyed, and learnt from. Facebook also has a useful 'Live' function where you can broadcast your experience direct to the pages of your friends and family. There has been a lot of criticism about Facebook and the way it is used to mine our personal data and sell products. Yet as a means of connection, communication and sharing when all else fails to work, it is a very useful tool indeed.

YouTube: This is a very large and ever growing video repository. When I first saw YouTube, I couldn't believe how simple it was to use. I also couldn't believe that there were so many videos I wanted to see. Some were humorous and entertaining, others thought provoking and challenging, and some were downright ridiculous. There is quite a lot of useless or unusable content on YouTube, just as there is on any user generated content site. Generally, content is not regulated, but to find the good content, you simply rely on the crowdsourced comments, likes and other user metrics to see which videos are the most useful. The video editing facilities now available on YouTube are quite sophisticated. To use them takes a little practice, but the results can be quite pleasing and YouTube certainly is a place where a lot of self-organised learning can occur.

Blogger: I saved the best until last. This is my favourite and most indispensable piece of my emergency rations kit. My blog is where all my ideas finally come together and are presented publicly. My blog is my engine house, used not only as a spur to action, where I know I have a ready global audience, but also a testing group or sand pit where I can test out new ideas and gain access to the views and alternative ideas of my own community of practice. Blogging has been demonstrated as a powerful method of learning from primary school children up to adulthood. Those who blog know they have an audience, and will generally raise their game to 'perform' their ideas to the best of their ability. Bloggers first must think of content that is interesting and relevant to their audiences, and then they need to craft its presentation (often after much personal research) into a style that is accessible and informative, often thought provoking or challenging, and in a format that is as free from error and as engaging as possible. This is no mean feat, and the most successful bloggers have developed their own formulae to sustain their audiences.

Each of the above tools has an array of social features that allow you to interact with others. This is the greatest appeal of these sites – the dialogical element that provides a rich social context within which content can be created, shared, discussed and repurposed. All the tools featured in this section are free to use and easy to use. And because they are virtually unlimited, none of them are rationed!

@kevin_corbett   **Kevin Corbett**

#edtech & #elearning program developer, Kevin Corbett is interested in #mlearning, #gamification & #socialmedia in education. Pacific Northwest, USA

When David asked me about my "Emergency rations: tech tools I couldn't live without" it immediately made me think of "The5 C's of Survival"[8].

I enjoy traveling and being on the go. Whether it's for business or pleasure, it's important when working in the technology industry to be connected, whether it's phone, email, text, or social media.

And while I am only too happy to unplug during special family times to stay focused and enjoy being in the moment, I'm not burdened and quite enjoy the power of anywhere / anytime access to the Internet & apps.

In preparation for an emergency, the notion of a "go bag" is an important consideration - what items must you have to survive? Wilderness survival experts, in considering the minimum items a person needs to withstand nature and the elements, generally start with the 5 C's: *Container, Combustion, Cordage, Cover, & Cut.*

If you've ever been asked to travel and present to a group, you know "survival" can be an accurate description because, you never know what you're going to be faced with when you reach your venue. I always want to be independent and prepared. In adapting the notion of 'The 5 C's of Survival', find below my technology "go bag".

Container: A while ago attendees at the Mobile Learning conference, hosted by Northern Arizona University and the Arizona K12 center, received a conference bag that years later is my favorite technology bag - it's fantastic! It has two lined and padded separate compartments for laptops & tablets: one for my Surface (productivity computer) and the other for my iPad (entertainment device). It also has a variety of other zipper & Velcro pouches for my awesome 2005 iPod Mini, Chromecast, cables & chargers. This small, lightweight, & functional bag has logged thousands of miles, having been with me to presentations around the United States and multiple trips to Asia. My Samsung Galaxy phone is always in my pocket at the ready.

Combustion: I'm not talking fire here, but the spark that makes technology come alive: electricity! In addition to device power supplies, I carry two, small, portable 20000mAh power packs that have multiple USB plug-ins for any device. I have my eye on a high-capacity solar charger for a purchase in the near future.

Cordage: Cords power, bind, tie, and build connections. Having the right cords in

---

[8] The 5 C's of Survival. *http://www.bushcraftspirit.com/five-c-of-survival/*

my tech bag are critical. I carry an assortment of charging cables, USB, and adapters for all of my devices. In addition, I always carry a 10' extension cord.

Cover: We're all familiar with coverage & its importance in connection. And we can always find a Wi-Fi hotspot…. or, can we? While perhaps excessive, I carry a Mi-Fi portable hotspot, from a different company than my cellphone, so I always have reliable connectivity and coverage.

Cut: In the survival sense, having a tool with which to cut is important for making things or to whittle away at something to create a new product. I've found that cloud-based storage (Google Drive & Dropbox) and associated tools help me cut out a lot of the technology I carry with me when a reliable connection is available. I've given large group presentations with only my Galaxy phone and a Chromecast. Powerful simplicity.

In conclusion, the emergency rations and technology tools I can't live without are summed-up as follows:

Kevin Corbett's 5 C's of Technology Survival:

- Container: small/lightweight, protective technology bag - holds my Microsoft Surface Pro, IPad, Chromecast & IPod.
- Combustion device: power sources & portable battery back-ups (solar too)
- Cordage: cables & cords of ALL kinds, for all devices.
- Cover: Mi-Fi
- Cut: Cloud-based storage & apps

@hopkinsdavid   **David Hopkins**

Teaching & Learning Consultant. @LearnAppeal trustee. Author 'The Really Useful #EdTechBook' and 'Emergency Rations: #EdTechRations' http://bit.ly/EdTechBooks. East Midlands, UK

I am certain that, had I more spare cash, I'd have collected more gadgets and wearables than I have. But, after reading some of the stories from the other contributors in this book, I feel quite glad I travel light. So light, in fact, it seems quite boring in comparison. Sorry. There are no cutting-edge gadgets or rare pocket game-stations (...yet! I've one on order from this Indiegogo crowdfunding campaign – the Spectrum Vega+[9]). There are, however, often overlooked items I could not live without - some you'll easily recognise as technology, some you'll suddenly think 'oh yes' as you remember that technology isn't only about something that's a year old. Or less.

Wearables
Glasses: I wear glasses/spectacles. All the time. These are fully functioning, help-me-to-see glasses. I can't take photos with them, but they help me to take amazing photos with either my phone or camera. They can't send email or tweet a friend or update Facebook, but they help me find whatever device I need so I can do it there. They can't drive a car or ride a bike or take my heart rate or call the doctor for me, but without them I'd be quite lost (literally).

Watch: I have a multi-functioning watch. It can tell the time, the date, and act as a stop-watch. It's clever enough that I don't need to wind it up, nor do I need to change its battery. It's solar powered; just a few hours in the sun will power it for a month or two. I've had it for about six years now and it's never caused me any problem - other than the stopwatch hand never points to top/12 anymore. It has the date, which is rarely right as I forget to wind the hours/days on in months with less than 31 days.

Rings: I have two rings, one wedding ring and another 'fashion' ring I picked up in a Madrid market for €6. The wedding ring has all the memories and life that can never be captured on anything other than my deep love for my family. I've had it resized once and should probably do so again (middle aged love of food), but it means so much more than just a gold band around my finger. When the days are long and tiring, it calms me down and lifts me up. When I'm lonely or confused, it offers comfort and love.

The other ring was a cheap metal two-coloured ring I bought on the spur of the moment, but it does remind me of one very special moment - at a conference in Madrid[10] I'd been invited to present at I realised it was the first time in my life I'd

---

[9] Sinclair ZX Spectrum Vega Plus console *https://www.indiegogo.com/projects/the-sinclair-zx-spectrum-vega-plus-console-games#/*

[10] 2014: EWMA Conference, Madrid.

been abroad. By myself. Without family, friends, wife, or work colleagues. Completely on my own. I had a day to spare between the opening of the conference and my sessions, so I took myself off into Madrid - no map, no Spanish, and just a few Euro's in my pocket. Twelve hours later I'd found my way to the centre, found a number of churches, a palace, a few cafés, an amazing ice cream parlour and a city bus tour. I watched street artists and life just go about its daily hustle and bustle. I found a magical plaza and watch an opera while eating a local ice cream and found a truly euphoric feeling of self-confidence I'd never had before.

The ring reminds me about treasures that are just around the corner if you stop what you're doing and take an unexpected left- or right-turn every once in a while. I rarely have the opportunity to take the road-less-travelled with work and home responsibilities, but every now and then, when the weekend has nothing planned for us, we sometimes go and do something different or new, or go somewhere we've never been before. It's so very low-tech but it's important to take stock of yourself once in a while, especially when everything else is so high-tech.

In my pocket
My pockets have the best tech possible. Coins. And a phone. Oh, and house/car keys.

iPhone: I have had a love affair with mobile phones since I got my first Panasonic in 1998[11]. I now have an iPhone 6S Plus, with leather flip cover that protects the corners (in case of a drop). I am forever needing to delete photos or apps to free up space for new stuff, and perhaps I should have gone for the larger 32gb model, but 16gb is what I've got. I was pretty sure I would not like the much larger body, but the extra screen helps my failing eyesight and now it's comfortable and familiar in my hand (until I need to use the keypad, then it's large and very uncomfortable for one-handed tapping) and the larger screen means I'm doing more on my phone where I used to use the iPad.

As with so many of these newer phones I baulked at the cost and tried to negotiate a shorter contract, but I've still got about 18 months left on the two-year contract (with an early upgrade option) so I treat it with respect and take care of it. My core apps are email, Twitter, camera, Safari, Instagram, Flipboard, Pinterest, Dropbox, WordPress, and more recently Slack and WhatsApp.

I swap games occasionally, but at the moment I have Monument Valley, Alto's Adventure, Outfolded, Blenduku 2 and Voi (check them out!). I use my phone as a camera a lot so tend to keep apps down to a minimum so I have storage space for family or trip photos, and I use the automatic backup to Dropbox all the time - this way I can delete them and free up storage quickly.

---

http://www.dontwasteyourtime.co.uk/conferences/2014-ewma/

[11] Reflection: My mobile phone journey.
http://www.dontwasteyourtime.co.uk/technology/reflection-my-mobile-phone-journey/

I have work and home emails loaded and sync'd. I am logged into various social apps like Twitter, Facebook, LinkedIn, Pinterest, Google+, etc. and I have a separate password manager and do not store passwords or financial of health details on my phone. I've only recently found the virtues of the newer tools like Slack and WhatsApp (embarrassingly it was my parents who got me trying it so we could keep in touch during their month-long trip to New Zealand. Me, jealous? Yup).

Notice anything yet...? That's right, the phone and SMS text features are not listed and are rarely used. So much for the core 'phone' in my pocket then, eh?

In my bag(s)
I have a day-bag to carry most things to and from work in (lunch, book, magazine/journal, etc.) as well as a man-bag (as someone described it last year) which I use when out and about with family or work - a great 'classic' bag from London Troop[12].

iPad: A little bashed around the edges (from where I dropped it on a marble floor of a restaurant in Madrid two years ago) and getting just noticeably slower to open apps and connect to the internet, but my iPad 4 still offers me that larger screen size from my phone when I want to do any volume typing that is just too hard on my iPhone.

Like so many I opted for the 16gb version, due to costs, so I feel I'm forever swapping and deleting apps to make room for something else. Ever since I got the iPhone 6S Plus I've found myself using the iPad less and less.

Powerbar: I found with my iPhone 4 (three or four years ago) that on a day out and I'd need to find a plug and recharge by about 3PM. Pretty useless when at country park or the middle of the New Forest. I now carry a fully charged Anker PowerCore+ with me everywhere. It's good enough a full charge on my iPhone 6S, or half a charge for my iPad.

Cables: I carry two cables with me pretty much all the time - USB-to-lightning cable for iPad and iPhone, and USB-to-micro connection that will work on both the Kindle and camera. These are also used by colleagues or friends at events who I inevitably meet who just happen to have forgotten their cables!

Notebook: Yes, the trusty notepad and pen. I have a couple of Moleskine notepads I keep on my desk: one for work, one for conference and event, and one for my work on other projects, like my books and my involvement as a trustee of a learning charity, Learn Appeal[13]. I haven't been able to get to grips with notetaking on phone or tablets, I have spoken to many who have extolled the wondrous freedom this gives, using apps like Evernote, but I've just not

---

[12] London Troop Bag. *https://www.instagram.com/p/6HvXOzRtj7/*

[13] Learn Appeal. *http://learnappeal.com/*

caught that bug yet.

Occasional use
Just because it's not with me all the time doesn't mean something isn't important or 'emergency', when I need it.

Kindle & books: I read books (yes, the paper variety) and eBooks (the Kindle variety). I've written about this before[14] that I am quite happy to change my use and preference for eBook over paper editions for different reading habits - work or pleasure. On my bedside table I have a couple of books on the go at the moment: Creativity Inc. by Ed Catmull[15] (a strongly recommended book for everyone who even remotely thinks their work is creative) and the 6-book Wolf Brother series by Michelle Paver[16]. I also have my Kindle where I'm reading the latest in the Ben Hope saga, by Scott Mariani, the Frontiers Saga, by Ryk Brown, and one of the many books on my '100 school book' project I've still yet to read[17]. Looking at this, I seem to lean towards books as part of a series, much like my TV viewing habit since getting a Netflix account!

Headphones: I have a set of in-ear headphones with me all the time, even though I rarely used them, but I keep a better pair of Sennheiser HD219's at home for more comfortable audio pleasure (also very useful when I want to watch House of Cards or Daredevil on Netflix, but my wife doesn't). These are also employed, like the Kindle, when I travel, even on day trips. They're not particularly small or portable, but they are on-ear rather than in-ear: I've found over-ear headphones make my ears too hot and I can't wear them for more than a few minutes before they get uncomfortable.

Camera: I recently bought a new camera, one designed to fit into my digital life and that would enable me to connect my phone or tablet to it, download the photos so I could share or upload to Dropbox. After much deliberation and chatting on Twitter I decided on the Sony HX90V[18] - 30x optical zoom, Wi-Fi connectivity (using the iOS app), and a variety of styles and compact body has made this one of my better purchases. I use the Sony iPhone app to backup photos to the phone, then upload to Dropbox and preserve the photos in case something happens to the camera.

---

[14] Books vs eBooks: it's about WHY as well as WHERE? *http://www.dontwasteyourtime.co.uk/ebook/books-vs-ebooks-its-about-why-as-well-as-where/*

[15] Creativity Inc. By Ed Catmull. *https://www.amazon.co.uk/dp/0593070097/*

[16] Michelle Paver - *http://www.michellepaver.com/wolf-brother/*

[17] 100 Books I'm going to read. *https://100schoolbooks.wordpress.com/*

[18] CameraLabs Sony HX90V Review. *http://www.cameralabs.com/reviews/Sony_Cyber-shot_HX90V/*

@jamesclay   **James Clay**

Drinks coffee and takes photographs of food. Oh, and does a bit with learning technologies too... Weston-Super-Mare, UK

@iLearningUK   Joel Mills

Learning Technologist of the Year, 2015. *http://bit.ly/LTAWinner*. *#MIEExpert #MinecraftMentor* educator, researcher, gamer & geek. Yorkshire, UK

I have broken my rations down into what I wear; devices I have on me at all times... day or night; devices in my pocket that I keep on me during the day, just in case; and my kit bag, stuff that gets hauled around from conference to hotel room, or from desk to home, but always contains things I might just need...

Wearables

Nike FuelBand: On my right wrist is my Nike FuelBand. My FuelBand measures how active I am during a day and uses a constructed unit of measure called "Nike Fuel", as well as the normal calories burned, steps taken etc. It has an LED point-light display that is activated by pressing a button and the various modes are then cycled through with additional presses of the button.

It connects to my iPhone 6+ via a Nike FuelBand app that uses Bluetooth to send data of my activity. The app produces beautiful infographics from my data and I can see when my active periods are and when I have been sat on my bottom for too long usually playing Minecraft! Interestingly, I am very active in the morning as I am up and about with our children, getting them dressed, breakfasts, packing bags for nursery, so I have a good 'spike' first thing before I get to work.

The down side of the FuelBand is that it is 'dumb'. If your activity does not include moving your wrist, it does not 'pick up' the activity. E.G. cycling... Also, resistance training, weight lifting, etc. might be burning off LOADS of calories, but as the wrist action is slow and the FuelBand has no idea of the weight you're lifting, it will give a false reading. Likewise, small wrist movements like driving a car will register a calorie burned, when in reality you are hardly using energy.

Some research was done on the accuracy of fitness trackers, and the FuelBand performed very poorly 'in real terms' in initial tests[19], calculating that I had burned more calories and taken more steps than I actually had.

However, using each day's data as a benchmark, I am able to see whether I have been more or less active than in previous days and therefore I am able to determine my activity levels. So it kind of works for me. I feel it is important piece of kit for me as the job has the potential to be very sedentary with long periods sitting at a desk staring at a screen, coding, testing, writing or reviewing.

Gamification of my life: This tool reminds me to be active and through the

---

[19] The Independent: Nike FuelBand owners to receive refund after lawsuit claims technology is inaccurate. *http://www.independent.co.uk/life-style/gadgets-and-tech/news/nike-fuelband-owners-to-receive-refund-after-lawsuit-claims-technology-is-inaccurate-10422103.html*

associated app and connected data with other Fuelband users, I can see how active I am compared to other people my age. Through this data, the rewards I get for being more active, for going on "3 day streaks" of smashing my target, of trying to get my "longest streak", my life becomes gamified and I am motivated... Occasionally not hitting my targets is very demotivating, but there is always a piece of cake to help lift the spirits... The Fuelband doesn't measure cake!

GameBand: I wear a Minecraft GameBand on my left wrist. My GameBand has working copies of Minecraft and MinecraftEDU[20] on it as well as saved games, and most importantly of all for a mobile educator, my Minecraft Education maps. Gameband allows me to simply plug-in and play Minecraft on any Mac or PC where I am presenting. I can run it from the USB and showcase what I need to, including a simple MinecraftEDU server. This means that without the need to cart my Laptop around, I can play, show and present Minecraft wherever I go. I have Minecraft, will travel! Oh, it's a USB key too (because I don't have enough of those...).

In my pocket
4GB & 8GB USB keys: You can never have too much storage.

64GB iPhone 6+: This has become my "go to" device for everything. It has largely replaced my iPad and is my social media tool of choice. My iPhone can do so, so much for teaching and learning. It keeps me connected to my networks through social media, through Skype, through Google Hangouts as well as the standard texts and occasional phone call.

The phone is my gathering and publishing device; I take pictures, record audio and video, stream from it, watch recordings on it, listen to it, take notes with it.

In my kit bag
MacBook Pro 15": My main computer. My workhorse. My friend. I have reached for a Mac for over 25 years now and it still is my preferred operating system to work on.

iPad 3 with retina display: Hardly used since the acquisition of an iPhone 6+. I find that there are still a few apps that I use on a regular basis that require the iPad. Apps like SpeedGrader are iPad only, whilst some apps like Evernote, FlipBoard and Paper by 53 are simply more enjoyable on the larger touch screen.

Logitec Wireless mouse: This doubles up as a wireless slide advancer for my Keynote presentations. I use Apple Keynote every time over PowerPoint. This also means I can Minecraft anywhere.

Apple earbuds with hands free mic (1st generation. The 2nd generation ones just fall out of my ears) x 2: For listening to podcasts, movies and music,

---

[20] Minecraft Edu - *https://education.minecraft.net/*

obviously. It also functions as an excellent recording mic for my own presentations, voice overs or interviews with people. Why two sets? I sometimes decant one set to my pocket, just in case!

Lightning to USB charging cable (non-Apple, flat, reinforced cable): essential for conferences and trains to recharge. Non-apple as you can get ones that are much more durable.

Lightning to VGA adapter: Essential to connect my MacBook Pro to any projector or lectern.

Lightning to Ethernet adapter: For when Wi-Fi speeds simply won't do, or Wi-Fi isn't available.

1m Ethernet cable: When Wi-Fi is password protected, often the Ethernet ports are not... Also, essential to hard-wire into routers for troubleshooting etc.

30 pin to USB charging cable: for now-largely-redundant iPad. Still comes in useful to lend to those in need of a charge.

30 pin to VGA adapter: for now-largely-redundant iPad. Handy for showing iPad apps in demonstrations when software Air-mirroring[21] won't work over Wi-Fi.

3.5mm Audio lead (male to male): Essential for taking sound from device to presentation AV kit. Can never rely on one being available at venue.

1st Generation iPod Shuffle (the chewing gum box): Handy for the gym, to save battery on phone, emergency tunes and oh... it too doubles up as a USB stick.

---

[21] Reflector 2. *http://www.airsquirrels.com/reflector/*

@iwilsonysj   **Ian Wilson**

Lecturer in Primary Education - Teaching with Technology in HE - interested in e-pedagogy and social media to support learning - Veggie - Soya Wet Latte pls. York, UK

Life would be easier with less devices and more implants. You might be a bit confused with this initial statement but there is some logic behind it. As far as I see it, we only have a limited number of places to put our devices and, even with this limited space, there is always the possibility of leaving something behind, dropping a device on the floor or even having it stolen. Once we have cybernetic implants then these possible events will become a thing of the past! However, until we evolve and enter the world of cyber-technology fully, I have to be content with a range of devices which I can keep as close to me as possible. My collection of the desirable devices is far from complete and only time, and some extra money will allow me to achieve my total ~~transformation~~ collection.

Physical Devices
iPhone 5S: Yes, I am still with the 5S. I have this routine that I upgrade every other model, starting originally with the 3S. I've had this 5S for a while and often looked with envy at some of the iPhone 6's functions. However, my envy will be coming to an end soon since, at the moment of writing this, I have just received an invitation for an upgrade, so an iPhone 7 might be on my belt soon. I say on my belt because, unusually, this is where phone lives. It has its own 'holster' and I whip it out when needed, like some sort of sheriff from the wild west. Yes, I do miss the holster at times when returning the phone and it ends up on the floor, but so far no damage. I don't have a watch so I use my phone for timekeeping as well, although as soon as I upgrade then the Apple Watch will definitely be purchased.

MacBook: Originally I purchased a MacBook Air but with the new style of MacBook's, the latter has become my carrying laptop of choice. Its compact and light enough to travel around with me in my backpack and has great processing speed. With Google Chrome installed I have access to my files on Google drive and it runs my essential applications (see below) allowing my data to be synchronise. It actually has the processing speed to run my screencast program, Screencast, and allows me to keep current with my mail and calendar items.

iPad: The final member of my trinity is the iPad. Although this has its own case, it shares my MacBook travelling case for ease of transport. I often have both my iPad and the MacBook out at the same time, with the MacBook being used for work and the iPad showing my to-do lists, emails or even running a Twitch Stream or video to keep me from getting bored. The iPad is also my go to device for Twitter and Facebook, when I don't want to get the MacBook out, and I take my video and images with it so that I don't drain my iPhone battery. Things sometimes just look better on a bigger screen.

Applications

Although my devices are paramount, I need them to support the applications which are essential for my functionality. These applications need to be able to be on every device and be able to synchronise across the now freely available Wi-Fi. Without these devices I would not be able to access my applications/data, but it is my applications which I would be completely lost without. These are definitely my emergency rations. I like to keep things simple so I only use three. Each have a specific function and work well together, reflecting my trinity of devices.

Google: If you have Google in your pocket the world is at your fingertips! Chrome is an excellent browser and signing into my Gmail allows my bookmarks to be synchronised between my devices.

Omnifocus: This is my task manager application[22]. I've tried other applications but nothing compares to Omnifocus for me. I can enter tasks into every device and they synchronise effectively reminding me when things need to be completed and even giving me prior warning of tasks to do.

Evernote: The final part of the trinity, this is my note taker. Coupled with the web clipper and Skitch[23], it allows me to capture notes, images, web pages and even sound wherever I am. Although initially I used to create specific notebooks for a storage system I have now moved onto using tags which is proving to be far more effective.

Last but not least

I wanted to use the concept of a trinity throughout this piece so unfortunately my last device got demoted into the 'and finally' section. Although not within the main trinity, it still has an important role to play in my rations.

iPod: I rarely take the car to work and with all the academic reading I have to partake in, I rarely read fiction books. The combination of these two events means that I listen to audiobooks. I mentioned the sometimes-limited battery life of my iPhone so I have kept with my iPod for my audiobooks and music. I go through a lot of 'ear buds' headphones mainly because of the way I miss treat them, stuffing them into my pocket and backpack.

So that's it! My double trinity of emergency rations. Although I will upgrade them and eventually add more wearables, they will probably remain unchanged for the foreseeable future. Until the advent of cybernetics and then I will be completely synchronised internally.

---

[22] Omnifocus - *https://www.omnigroup.com/omnifocus*

[23] Evernote Skitch - *https://evernote.com/skitch/*

@neilwithnell   **Neil Withnell**

Mental Health Nurse, Senior Fellow HEA. Associate Dean Academic Enhancement. Cyclist. *#LTHEchat* Golden Tweeter Award holder *#LSP #byod4l*. Salford, UK

I have never dashed out or queued up for the latest gadget, I tend to await reviews and take my time in choosing, but I do like gadgets!

Looking through my modest collection I have the following, in no particular order:

Laptop: A trusty old Asus X501A that I often take with me, but find that it is rarely used. It has never let me down when the need has arisen, but find that this tends to be a fallback when all else fails. I bought this to replace a desktop, as the need to be more mobile and flexible makes my life so much easier.

Tablet(s): I own two IPad's now, as the older version seemed to slow down (probably due to overuse, the newer version won't be that far behind!) I use every day, almost as much as the iPhone. My first iPad was a gift and I instantly loved it. The ease of use, instant connectivity and size suits me to the ground. I also own a Samsung Galaxy Tab 4 - not a purchase but won in a competition. I have started to play around with this to become more familiar with the android apps, having been very Apple biased so far.

Mobile phone: I am still on the iPhone 5S as this is fairly new to me having had the 4 for some years. I opted for Apple and as a consequence was bought the iPad, they both sync and this makes my life so much easier. The iPhone is a "must-have with me at all times" gadget (well almost all the time) as this not only keeps me in touch with the world, but organises my life. The calendar informs and reminds me where I need to be and at what time, and the various notifications (although can be often annoying) are usually helpful. The number of apps is way too many, but I don't delete as I worry that I may need that app one day. Email tends to be the most used part of the phone at number 1, followed very closely by Twitter, with the lowest on the list being the phone call facility (why call it a phone?)

Reader: I like to read and find myself completely lost when immersed in my kindle, so much so that I have been known to miss the stop on the train. The screen is amazing, having spent many days in the sun this has always been crystal clear, a worthwhile investment.

Google cardboard: This is new to me (and only £5), but I find myself becoming very keen to develop Virtual Reality (VR) in my teaching. I have used Augmented Reality (AR) and find the benefits of this extremely rewarding. I see a huge future in VR and AR, and no doubt will be adding Oculus (or more likely) HoloLens[24] to this collection.

---

[24] Microsoft HoloLens - *https://www.microsoft.com/microsoft-hololens/en-gb*

Headphones: I have lost count as to how many headphones I have; they tend to be the cheaper versions but suit me adequately well. I have three sets in my bag (don't ask) as I do enjoy listening to music, watching videos and joining in Skype and Google Hangout conversations - a great way to collaborate from wherever I am.

Sports gadgets: I like sports and have always been fairly sporty. I don't compete as much now, but I do enjoy cycling and (not as much) running. I own a Garmin 520 for cycling, which is a great piece of kit. This has maps and lets me know how 'slow' I am riding, distance travelled and also live segments so that I can compete with myself and others. My running watch is a Garmin 200 which I have had for many years.

Battery charger: I cannot function without this, a very well used Recharge 2500. This can give 'me' enough power to get through the day no matter where I am, I just have to remember to charge it the day before!

Power cables: Owning so many devices, I need various cables to plug them into a mains outlet, providing there is a mains outlet.

@amyburvall   Amy Burvall

The Cloud is Our Campfire. Learning & Creative Thinking consultant; professional recombinant connecting dots; History Music Vids *@historyteacherz*. Oahu, Hi. USA

Canadian media philosopher Marshall McLuhan proposed that technology is an extension of the self. My smartphone has become just that. In the past year, I have purposefully tried to do everything I need or desire to do on my iPhone 6+: that goes for productivity and creativity. The large screen allows me to work without the use of a stylus (though my preferred stylus is 'Pencil' made by Fifty-Three[25]).

I find that I sketch better, for example, when I rely on what I call my "raw fingers" ...perhaps it is the visceral experience, or something that hearkens wild abandon. Personally, I love both digital and analogue technology, and I never forget that physical paper and a pen is indeed "technology".

My external memory rests on hundreds of slips of unlined paper - everything from the backs of receipts to luxurious leather-bound notebooks. My phone is used primarily for connections and creations - it allows me to have "ambient intimacy" with those I love and learn from who live oceans away. This collage highlights my essentials for working, making, and living:

---

[25] Pencil by Fifty-Three: *https://www.fiftythree.com/pencil*

Image / Centre:

"Technology as an extension of the self" M. McLuhan

Paper app by Fifty-Three: This is my go-to app to end all apps, and I can confidently say it has changed my life and career. It is so intuitive and simple compared to other drawing apps. I try to hack the ways in which it can be used, and find the fact that one can sketch over an imported image perfect for my remix endeavors. I often take screen shots of things I'm reading and use the pen tools to annotate, saving later for potential blog posts. Lately I've been creating stop-motion animation by duplicating and adjusting sketches slightly, then splicing as a gif.

Image / Left:
IPhone 6+: When my previous iPhone cracked, I debated purchasing a 6+ or a smaller phone plus iPad Pro. I came to the conclusion that the best camera / sketchbook / fill-in-the-blank is the one you have with you, and decided to go with the large screened 6+. The canvas size eliminates my need for a stylus and frankly, I'm getting on in years so large is lovely. Most used feature? The camera. In fact, I use my phone as a camera more than as a phone. Did you know the camera makes an excellent magnifying glass? If I can't read the fine print on a medicine bottle or credit card it is simply a matter of taking a shot and zooming!

WhatsApp: Vying for first place with Twitter as my most-used app for connection, WhatsApp is perfect for cost-effective communication with all my friends living in far off lands (which is pretty much everyone since I reside in the middle of the Pacific Ocean). I use the voice message and video functions quite often, and I love how certain messages can be starred for later perusal.

Twitter: Twitter is my all-time favourite social media platform both as a web and mobile app. I hesitate to admit it is the first thing I check upon waking in the morning. I love the creative constraints of 140 characters (though that has changed recently) and the fact that it allows for serendipitous connection, particularly if you can leverage a hashtag. I try to use images in about 85% of my tweets. I love how it plays well with other apps, such as the blogging platform Medium, where you can highlight excerpts from a post and Twitter privileges the screenshot.

I used Twitter extensively with my high school students as a backchannel, for socratic discussions, to amplify their work, and to pose and track a "question of the week". Personally, I've developed several collaborative creativity projects that involve volleying artistic responses back and forth with others, or crowdsourcing work.

Google Plus: While it seems like no one uses Google Plus, I could not live without G+ Communities. I have created open communities for several topics in which I'm interested, including Emerging Literacies, Remix in the Classroom, Visual

Literacy and Creativity. They have become my bookmark warehouse, my curation centre. I love how they function like other social media, with comment threads and the most current post at the top, yet have a "web site feel" because content can be organized by category (not to mention hashtags!). During workshops, I invite participants to join, and they can have access to all front-loaded resources whilst contributing their own artifacts. After the event is over the conversation continues as the community flourishes.

Slack: This chat app fosters affinity spaces. There is a certain freedom of expression in these semi-private backchannels, and I'm thrilled to belong to a few I access on a daily basis. The one thing I don't care for is the linear stream...it is a bit difficult when reading a reply to have to search all the way back up the thread to find the original. I do love how gif-friendly it is, as many of my friends tend to communicate using these animated morsels.

Wordpress: Aside from amplifying my thoughts, blogging helps me to do the thinking. I pay for the use of customization since I feel maintaining a consistent colour palette helps one's digital presence. But sometimes I'm not ready to write - in these cases, I plop down the relevant inspiration (links, random ideas, title concepts, etc.) and save as a draft. Right now, I have about 15 unwritten blog ideas but they will be there when I can get to them. Composing a blog post can be daunting, so something that helped me was to assign a category called #Rawthoughts. These are much briefer and exemplify something I call "fleenking", a portmanteau of "fleeting thinking". Most importantly, I design several original images per post so that I can "chunk" the text for easier digestion and add catchy subtitles.

Screenshot: This is probably my most used "feature" on any device. Clive Thompson[26] has written about the dominance of the screenshot in internet culture. Sometimes I snip quotes from articles, though most of my shots are images.

Instagram: I use Instagram as archival repository of all my artwork and travel photos. Automatic cross-posting is not for me, as some things are more appropriate for Twitter and others for Facebook. But Instagram is my catch-all. The one major letdown is that it is difficult to search your own feed to retrieve that one needed image. I get around this by creating relatively unique hashtags (usually an original portmanteau) for my projects. This app is a constant source of creative inspiration for me - while I do follow quite a few friends, the bulk of my feed is derived from interesting artists and designers, and I use the recommended search to find more intriguing posts on a daily basis.

YouTube: I fell in love with YouTube in its early days as I gained some recognition posting my history-based music video parodies there. YouTube is my Google - I use it more for search and for learning, though I rarely write comments or even

---

[26] 'The most important thing on the Internet is the screenshot' by Clive Thompson: https://www.wired.com/2015/03/clive-thompson-6/

favourite videos. Playlists were quite handy when I was teaching, and I once gave an entire exam based on viewing and analysing videos in thematic playlists. I truly think having a YouTube channel is, for students, as essential as having an email address as it facilitates the making and sharing of vlogs and video projects as well as the curation of resources. I find YouTube Editor quite handy for adding copyright-free music tracks to my animations.

Notebooks: Nothing quite beats a notebook for pinning down one's butterfly-like ideas. I ONLY purchase non-lined paper notebooks and I do fancy a whimsical cover. Just like my high school days, most pages are littered with random doodles, making my notebooks more of an ode to medieval monk marginalia than anything else.

Envelopes and Other Random Slips of Paper: I inherited my tendency to re-purpose scratch paper from my grandmother, whose frugality stemmed from living through two world wars and the Great Depression. When ideas hit you, you need the quickest source of paper you can get, and often that is a crumpled receipt in the bottom of my handbag. I love the thickness of envelopes and often use the backs of discarded ones that formerly delivered bills to jot down thoughts whilst in a Skype meeting or to brainstorm a keynote talk. The odd length of an envelope lends itself perfectly for list making, which is something I do at the beginning of each day.

Ultra-Fine Sharpie (black): You will never catch me with a ball-point pen. I exclusively use felt tip and prefer the ultra-fine Sharpie brand. Japan makes some pretty fab pens, so it is a frequent treat of mine to pop into our local Japanese stationery store and pick up a few new ones (Sakura Gelly Roll[27] especially).

Image / Right:
Phone charger: Never leave home without it. I like to keep my charger in a mesh jewelry bag and decorate it with Japanese washi tape (currently in faux black lace).

Quotations (usually Goodreads): A lot of my work is based on curating and synthesizing existing ideas, and I love learning from great thinkers and artists of the past. Quotations are very dear to me. I love the way they can be short yet poignant, and often open to multiple interpretations. I sketch them often, particularly in response to a current event or famous figure's birthday (I call these #sketchquotes). My favourite app for finding quotes from a specific person or about a target topic is Goodreads. You can tweet these directly out but recently I've been taking screenshots of the quote, uploading the text image to Paper by Fifty-Three, and decorating around them.

Black suede lace-up heeled boots: I travel a lot and need a perfect shoe that will work with dresses or pants, casual or fancy, and be funky and stylish yet

---

[27] Sakura Gelly Roll pen: *https://www.gellyroll.com/*

comfortable. I've found that in a pair of black suede boots that zip up the side for easy take-off when I'm...taking off (as in at the airport security).

Uber: Aside from London, where I fancy taking black cabs, Uber is my best friend when travelling. The best part in my opinion is the sense of control and peace of mind one achieves whilst following the driver's status before the pickup. I would almost consider not visiting places that don't have Uber. Besides, most drivers offer bottled water, mints, and phone chargers for all your emergency needs.

United Airlines: For a few years, I have flown solely on one airline (recommended because it will lead to preferred status with faster check-in, more luggage allowance, and frequent upgrades). I book all my tickets, check flight status, review mileage and upgrade announcements, and obtain in-flight internet all from one app. Now if it only played Gershwin...

Moo business cards: This is the best business card production company ever. Moo cards are recognizable a mile away. They are printed on thick, luxe recycled paper and are usually rounded at the corners, like an app! Actually, they come in all different shapes and sizes including square a la Instagram and "mini". The best part is their "Printfinity" feature which allows for a different image to be printed on each card in a deck. Recipients seem to love the choice (I keep my decks at about 10 unique images), and one of my friends wanted to "collect them all!". This would be perfect for designers, artists, and photographers to showcase their entire portfolio in a deck. I've purchased Moo stickers and postcards for branding and as giveaways at conferences.

Perfume (travel size): Never exit the front door without spare perfume - I prefer the travel size roll-on of my favourite scent. More impromptu interesting conversations have started because someone asks me what perfume I'm wearing.

Lipsticks: I'm a big believer in the power of lipstick - if you have no other makeup, lipstick will suffice. I carry with me at least two shades - a bold blueish red (which gives the optical illusion of whiter teeth) and a something in the rose-pink family which is neutral and natural, yet completes a polished look.

Passport and Global Entry card: I once stated cheekily I'd never date a man without a passport. Nothing says "let's whisk away to the Riviera tomorrow" like a valid passport. Better yet if you can obtain dual citizenship or multiple passports. I've bolstered mine a bit with the best $100 I've ever spent - my Global Entry card. This gives me preferred status at airports in the U.S. and Canada when I travel internationally, allowing me to bypass those long customs and security lines.

Cat Eye sunglasses: Sunglasses are more than fashion, they are protection...they are mystique...they are preventative anti-aging treatment! I wear them in all-weather to cut down on glare and never exit the front door without at least two pairs. I prefer vintage looking cat eyes and never spend much money on them because, let's face it, they are all plastic, easy to lose, and someone will most likely end up sitting on them. There is no more effective eye wrinkle elixir!

@MarenDeepwell   Maren Deepwell

CEO @A_L_T | leadership and CPD in Learning Technology, all things open, innovation, large scale learning & teaching... | also tweeting #altc #cmalt. UK

The things that I cannot do without have become fewer and smaller over time. In part that is thanks to the advances in minimisation and technological innovation in general. My smartwatch can now do most things I used to use my phone for and my phone can now do most of what I used to do on a laptop or tablet. Yet there are still some things that I take everywhere, ready for whatever the day might bring.

As is becoming increasingly common, my place of work can vary a lot from day to day and mostly I work on the go, between meetings or on the way to give presentations. I don't often meet people I work with closely face to face. Still, I have to be able to collaborate effectively, so most of the technology I can't do without helps me to keep in touch and to work together.

Chromebook & Google apps for Education
For about two years now a basic Toshiba Chromebook has been my constant companion. Bought initially to provide short term support during large events I have ended up using it for everything.

As a piece of kit, it certainly has its limitations. For me there are significant advantages: to start with it is cheap, robust and data is not stored on the device so I cannot lose it. It starts up quickly, it is easy to use and provided you either learn or know how to use the apps, it runs it delivers a great user experience. I have learnt some short cuts that really make a difference and the support documentation online is constantly growing. I am very partial to the mobile devices I have running iOS because I prefer the user interface, but on the laptop Android does a good job and is constantly improving.

Having limitations in what I software I can use has also had two other benefits: first, it has made my work more collaborative as practically everything I work on is shared. Secondly. It has forced me to take a simpler approach to complex tasks. I like the elegant simplicity I have become accustomed to.

I use as many different operating systems as possible because I like to keep in touch with what iOS/MacOS, Android and Windows feel like. Google apps for Education help me switch between different devices and operating systems (nearly) seamlessly. Becoming more expert at using and administrating GAFE has had the welcome additional benefit of enabling me to support colleagues across the organisation better.

Pen & paper
However much I use my watch, phone or laptop, I use pen and paper every day and it is something I could not do without. It doesn't matter what kind of digital technology I have at my disposal there are always times when putting pen to

paper is my first choice. Drawing, sketching, writing - there's no substitute for me. I have a green Moleskine notebook that I take everywhere and solutions to some of the most complex things I do at work start life as a scribbly drawing on the pages of that notebook marked clearly by the uneven movement of the train.

Headset, mobile data storage, power packs
Other bits and pieces that I usually have somewhere in my bag are a headset or headphones, a variety of options for data storage big and small and also at least one power pack to charge up mobile devices. I am not very good at carrying around the right kind of adapters for various things, so I rely on being able to plug in my Chromebook and everything else has to survive the day without top up. I am not choosy about which particular make I have as too often these small items get borrowed by co-presenters or colleagues and end up to need replacing.

Business cards, flyers or other printed materials
I work with many people who are skeptical about Learning Technology or indeed technology in general. No matter what the context is there is always someone who prefers to have paper in their hand. So, in that instance all of the digital technology I carry around can be useless and I have to have some form of paper back up. Business cards or printed postcards or flyers can be useful here. They are also a good alternative for when the technology or connectivity let me down. And you never know who you might meet on a train.

Shoes...
However much I work virtually, walking places is a major part of my working life. Sometimes it is simply between one room and another within a conference venue, on other days it is through a new city. My watch or phone might be measuring the distance or help me navigate along my route, but clocking up the miles is hardest on my feet. Shoes that are still comfortable 12 hours into my day and get me as fast as possible from A to B are essential. Shoes can say a lot about a person. They are part of making a first impression, everyone sees them when you stand on stage or at the front of a lecture theatre. Just like stickers on a laptop or pin badges on lapels shoes can make a statement about who you are and where you are going.

@suebecks   **Sue Beckingham**

Educational Developer/Senior Lecturer/SFHEA at @sheffhallamuni. Researching social media. @Hootsuite_UK Ambassador @BYOD4L @LTHEchat. Sheffield, UK

When considering my choice of emergency items - the items I cannot possibly go without on a daily basis - it got me thinking about if and how our personality might affect our shopping habits. How do traits like being decisive, cautious, curious and adventurous impact on the way we shop for and then engage with technology?

- **The Decisive Shopper:** knows exactly what she wants and goes to the store, locates the item, buys it and leaves.
- **The Cautious Shopper:** often hesitant and will ponder, not necessarily making a decision until opinions are sought.
- **The Curious Shopper:** spends a lot of time exploring different items
- **The Adventurous Shopper:** loves to try new things and known to buy on impulse

Indulge me here whilst I take this a bit further. We don't buy technology every day or even every week, but we all buy food. Our food shopping habits might portray us as:

- **Just in time buyers:** last minute to fulfil immediate needs
- **Organised:** weekly replenishment and a planned shopping list
- **Bargain hunters:** after the latest special offer
- **Scouts** (be prepared): extra supplies prior to public holidays or impending severe weather
- **Hoarders:** multiples of everything
- **Indulgers:** special treats or big spenders on those often calorific non-essentials

The Larder
What goes in your larder can depend on the kind of shopper you are. Available time to shop and cash to spend, the time of year, increased work commitments, impending visitors and other factors are also likely to affect your shopping habits and therefore what you have on your shelves. Access to power and the size of your fridge and freezer will determine what you can store. Recipe books, cooking programs, friends and new healthy living regimes can all influence what you buy.

The Emergency Ration Pack
When you think of the term emergency rations you'd be forgiven for thinking of those food items that you buy in case of emergency when partaking in some outward-bound activity – water, chocolate, meat jerky, nuts. But think about the items you habitually use. On a daily basis I pack my emergency rations to get me through the day at work, avoiding the need to go out and buy supplies at inflated prices. Ration packs need to be compact and light to carry, nutritious, and where

no access to a kitchen, ambient (no refrigeration needed) and ready to eat. Typically, this might be a sandwich but I am often influenced to try new things by observing what my peers eat.

So, applying the food analogy to my use of technology, let me share with you what I currently have in my 'Tech Larder' and the items I must have with me in my 'Tech Emergency Ration Pack' (aka cannot go out without).

My Tech Larder
The items in my larder have increased considerably over the last couple of decades. Looking back to the late 90s as a family we shared a desktop PC and a landline telephone. Dial up internet meant we could choose to use one or the other, but not both at the same time. Before long we all acquired mobile phones, which were then upgraded to smartphones. Wi-Fi gave us all 24/7 access to a whole new online experience. As prices came down, laptops replaced the desktop and in time we each had our own. A combined wireless printer and scanner serves us all. New apps like Skype enabling video chat required webcams and headsets, but then were made redundant as replacement laptops had these integrated within them. Streaming entertainment and the use of headphones meant we could engage in individual interests whilst sitting in the same room. Multiple devices required additional multi-way plug extension sockets to keep our devices charged. Portability became a focus and iPads and tablets became desirables, providing extra screen size our smartphones didn't have, and yet were still light to carry around. From 3G to 4G, mobile contracts gave us access to the internet wherever there was a signal and as we became 'forever switched on'; battery packs provided power back up when we were out and about. A solar pack kept my phone going when I spent 5 days trekking across the Sahara Desert!

So, in my tech larder I have amassed a variety of items. Some are used daily, others sporadically, and there is a collection of items laid to rest in the loft as I haven't yet had the heart or inclination to dispose of them.

I'd consider myself as a Curious Tech Shopper (spends a lot of time exploring different shops) usually doing so online. My interest in technology is often piqued by the devices my peers have, articles and reviews I read online, and a network I can reach out to and find out more. My shopping habits for technology are multiplex:

- **Organised**: in the main I'll replace items only when needed
- **Bargain hunter**: it's sometimes a challenge to miss out on a special offer
- **Scout (be prepared)**: the battery pack, extra batteries, spare pencils and, if space, a multi-way plug extension in case sockets are in short supply are all essentials when away from home
- **Hoarder**: find it hard to throw things out, rather than multiples of the same device
- **Indulger**: always tempted by upgrades ... and I would add
- **Window shopper**: I have a list as long as my leg of things I'd like to buy!

My Tech Emergency Ration Pack

Now to get to the point of this chapter, what tech would I consider as essential items in my emergency rations? If I had to gather the most cherished items I use every day into one bag I could carry with me, here is what I would include and why each is important.

Smartphone: For years, I cherished my neat and compact Nokia, but with advent of the smartphone I chose the iPhone and have never looked back. Within this amazing device I can access a phone, address book, email, clock, timer, calculator, camera, video, notes, reminders, voice memos, music, compass, map, and of course the Internet. To add to this, I can download a multitude of apps which provide direct links to the social networks I engage with, interactive bus and train timetables, news and shopping sites, and a whole host of other apps that inspire productivity, creativity, and collaboration, as well providing access to entertainment and informal learning. I use my phone a lot so taking its charger is a must. As access to power might be an issue I've recently invested in a Recharge battery charger to provide emergency power.

Laptop: My current laptop is an HP Pavilion which comes with a built-in webcam. I chose a 15-inch screen and find this a nice size to work with. It fits nicely into a Built neoprene laptop bag, the spongy handles making it comfortable to carry. I've not really taken to solely using the touchpad and prefer a mouse. The HP Wireless Z4000 Mouse is slim and a useful travel companion. My preferred browser is Chrome and I've added my frequently used sites to settings so they auto-launch when I open the browser. Battery life is good but the charger has to come with me if I intend to use the laptop throughout the day.

Tablet: If I want to travel lighter, then I may forgo taking my laptop and charger for an IPad Mini. This is just a bigger version of my smartphone (minus the phone) but is easier on the eye. I'm looking for an integrated keyboard/case as for prolonged use I'd find this preferable to the touch screen. A neoprene cover keeps it protected. It shares the same charger I use for my iPhone.

Pen drive and External hard drive: Whilst I use Google Drive and Dropbox for collaborative work, I tend to store items I'm working on and photos on a pen drive, then back this up on an external hard drive. This habit stemmed from the need to access saved items offline. Technology is moving on, and it's now possible to view and edit files using Google Drive offline, and then sync the new version once you have access to Wi-Fi. (Tip: You must be connected to the Internet to turn on offline access.) I'm still reluctant to let go of the pen drive and external hard drive but sometime soon I should.

Kindle: Whilst I could access eBooks on other devices I have, in the sunshine the screens are not reader friendly. The Kindle is small and compact and can easily slip into my bag, providing a source of reading. Battery life is good but taking the charger is a must if away for a few days.

Moleskine notebook and Papermate Non-Stop mechanical pencil: I still love to write and doodle by hand and rarely leave home without some kind of notebook and pencil. Believe me I've had numerous notepads in various shapes, sizes, designs and colours but my Moleskine has become my favoured one. It is sturdy and the elastic band keeps it closed. I have an A6 version for notes and A5 versions (in different colours) for work and studying. I write with a pencil and go for the mechanical pencil with rubber attached. I'm left handed and not the neatest of writers. Ink smudges.

My daily productivity increases when I have access to technology. I can utilise the time commuting to and from work, or indeed wherever I am. Access to the Internet and my personal learning network has opened my eyes to numerous ways technology can be applied. Curiosity and the willingness to experiment in the knowledge help is always at hand is what I feel has made my 'emergency ration tech pack' so valuable.

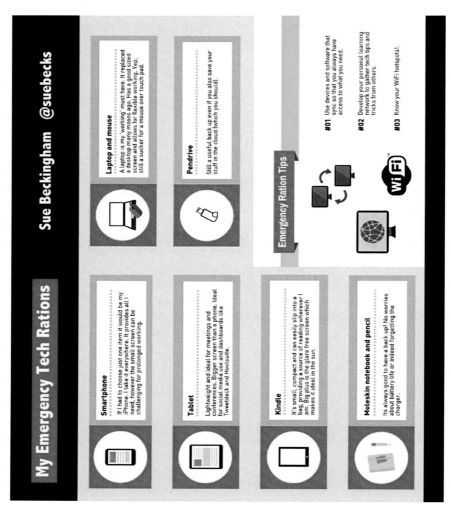

@JackieCarter   **Jackie Carter**

Senior Lecturer and Director for Engagement with Research Methods Training. Manchester, UK

I was asked to write this piece at a time when my house had just been flooded. As a result, we had to move out whilst the repairs were undertaken. As someone who travels a lot with work and is pretty much surgically attached to her devices, I became acutely aware suddenly of the need to be selective in what I carried in my 'day bag'. Here is what I discovered.

In my bag & pockets

Phone: I use an iPhone 6. I've had iPhones for about 6 years now and consider myself device agnostic but do love its simplicity. I flit between all the social media apps - Twitter, Facebook, LinkedIn and WhatsApp on a regular basis, often forgetting who contacted me on which App. I read work and personal emails on it (I have 3 work accounts and 2 personal ones). The calendar (available on all my devices) regulates my life - if it's in the calendar I attend, if it's not I don't - whether professional or personal.

I couldn't get to where I'm going without my phone - so I no longer print out maps of meetings but instead completely and utterly rely on there being Wi-Fi connection so I can navigate to any location on Google Maps. Plus, I book travel using TheTrainLine app and travel around London with my London Tube Map app.

I use other apps for booking and finding out about non-work related stuff; Shazam, Goodreads, Cineworld, IMDB. I use my phone to create content, mostly photos but also videos, which sometimes get uploaded to YouTube. I don't use it for editing documents other than notes (I've taken to keeping my to-do lists on it). And, of course, now I have a Spotify subscription I play music off it too. I recently stayed (as a result of the flood!) at a younger friend's house and was thrilled to discover the delights of streaming Spotify through her speaker system. I still find the battery life less than completely satisfactory, but carry a plug so I can always charge up, and sometimes (if I remember and can find it) a mobile charger.

And yes I do use it as a phone. I make a receive a fair amount of calls (my role includes the title 'engagement' so I spend a lot of time 'engaging'.

Looking back at this list I can see how instrumental to my life (work and personal) this little device is. It's perhaps time I learned to go beyond the one finger typing I use!

Laptop: My laptop is part of me too. It's a MacBook Air, 13 inch, and I use it daily. I take it to all work meetings, and mostly use it to read and write emails, create documents and do my job. The browser is always open with at least 5 tabs (usually many more but I'm trying to get better at closing things after use).

Interestingly I've much less to say about my laptop than my phone, although I spend a significant part of my day on it. I used to use Dropbox and sync all my files and folders but no longer do, and I miss it. I've taken to using Google Drive, which I like but requires an Internet connection. As already noted I travel a lot for work and take my laptop almost always. It's a little battered now (from an internal flight overhead locker) but it does what I need it to. And I use it for entertainment too - Netflix and Amazon video - mostly when I am travelling.

Tablet: I use an iPad, but less frequently than my laptop. If I'm travelling light I tend to take it with me but find that the applications on the iPad are not really fit for purpose, though they no doubt exist so it's probably a case of my not having found them yet. I mainly use the iPad for reading books and watching media.

Notebook and pens: As well as the phone and laptop, which I usually place side by side in meetings, I also still use paper and pen. I find this is what I tend to refer back to when I make 'notes to myself'. Also, because I do a lot of work with math's and stats I prefer pen and paper for working things out. My notebook accompanies me to most work activities.

Pencil case: I think this must be a throwback to my teaching days, but my pencil case includes pens, a USB stick, my iPhone charger and of course pens. I misplace pens frequently.

Work pass: I think this counts as technology. My work pass allows me to enter and leave the car park, pay for refreshments at work, and enter and leave designated buildings which require access - including the library. I carry it on a lanyard but no longer wear it so am usually digging through my handbag for it. I'm not sure why I don't wear it any more as I used to - perhaps it's because no one else does where I work now.

Watch: I wear a watch, a battery powered watch, for which I now have a life-long guarantee (for the battery, not the watch). Although I have many devices which would enable me to tell the time I still like wearing a watch. This particular one was a gift on my half-century birthday.

FitBit: I've included this here, not because it's an essential part of my daily attire but because it should be. I wore a Fitbit daily about a year ago. It broke, I got a new one, but life was busy and I failed to set it up. Since then I have done less daily exercise and because I can ignore it (no daily reminders about numbers of steps done) I have become lazier. That's not to say I am lazy - far from it, I'm active, busy, fit (the amount of exercise I can do shows I have stamina) - but I have chosen to ignore the quantification of my regular exercise.

My reflection is that, in actual fact, I use a limited number of applications and apps on my devices, and am probably in need of an update for some of them. My most essential device is my iPhone and MacBook. On the occasions when II am without it for any length of time I've missed it. Not quite as much as missing a child, but not far off.

@Chri5rowell   Chris Rowell

LT Specialist, Socialist, ALT editor, South of the River - My tweets are my own views...well except for the ones RTed! Camberwell, UK

With age comes reading glasses! I only started wearing glasses for reading a couple of years ago and I'm still getting used to them. Because I don't need them all the time the problem is not wearing them but remembering where I left them. I have often been looking for them only to find them in my top pocket or on my head, this has often caused me loads of embarrassing when I've asked a colleague "has anyone seen my glasses?".

What I like about modern technology, especially the mobile phone, is that it's meant that I can ditch the only piece of technology I used to wear, my watch. I never felt comfortable wearing a watch but as a lecturer I couldn't do without it. Having a mobile phone in the classroom with a stopwatch and timer meant that I could more easily keep time and coordinate classroom activities.

In my pocket
Before my Grandfather left the house, he used to make the 'sign of the cross' and recite the phrase "spectacles, testicles, wallet and watch". It was just a simple way to remind himself that he'd got everything he needed for the day. My modern-day version is to replace 'watch' with 'phone':

Phone: The phone I use all the time is a Motorola Moto 4G (3rd Generation). I don't really have any brand loyalty when it comes to phones. Over the years, I've moved from Nokia to Blackberry to the iPhone and finally to my current Motorola handset. Moving away from the iPhone phone was a big decision for me. I really liked the simplicity and reliability of the Apple phones but I just needed a bigger screen as the ravages of old age started to affect my eyesight. Having a 5-inch screen means that I don't have to scramble around my bag to find my glasses and I can use the GPS maps on my bike when I'm traveling to a new location.

Keys: There are two things that I have on my key ring that are on my essentials list. One is my Santander bike hire key. I only use this occasionally but it's a handy option living in London. After paying a one-off fee of £3 for the key its gives me quicker access to the bikes and Pay As You Peddle membership. Great for when my bike's off road or I'm visiting an unknown part of London and don't want to leave my own bike in an unknown part of London. The second gadget I have on my key ring is my 'I LOVE ORKNEY' bottle opener, a souvenir from my holiday last summer. I bought it from the Tourist Information shop in Kirkwall when I was stranded with a bottle of 'Northern Lights' and no way of opening it. I've used it on countless times since last summer – an essential!

Nello bike bell: The one other item that I have is my favourite bit of new technology. However, it's no ordinary bike bell. Cycling in London is a hazardous affair, avoiding cars is main concern but avoiding pedestrians looking at their phones is more common occurrence. The Nello Bike Bell[28] has 3 very loud tones and is also magnetic so I can take it off my bike and keep it in my pocket. It also means the bell is disabled when it's unconnected from the bike.

In my bag(s)

I have two bags that I use on a regular basis. One is my cycling rucksack which I use on my regular commute to work. The other is my 'pedestrian' bag which again I use for work and conferences. The cycling bag consists of all my cycling 'All bells and whistles'...

Before 'Learning Technology' became an entity, cyclists were the leading connoisseurs of technology and gadgetry. My essential cycling tech consist of:

B'TWIN Tyre lever set: Cheap and cheerful, very sturdy, never let me down.

Zefal Micro hand pump: Amazingly only 16cms long and weighing in at 8g I hardly know it's in my bag.

Revolution Tune up multi-tool: The 'Swiss Army Knife' for cyclists. With these 3 items, I can face any eventually the London roads inflict upon me.

The other bag I have is manly used for work and conferences when I'm not on my bike:

Hewlett Packard Notebook: I still rely on my trusty Notebook when I need to type up meeting/conference notes or access my blog to edit or write a new post. I still feel that I need the full QWERTY keypad when I'm writing more than a few sentences.

Betron Earphones Headphones: Again, not the most expensive in-ear headphones but they give me decent enough sound quality – I'm a massive music fan and regularly access the BBC Radio app (Radios 4 & 6) and my Amazon Music app where most of music is stored.

Anker PowerCore+ mini Portable Charger: Even though the battery life on my Motorola phone is much better than a iPhone I still need a back power supply. There is nothing worse than a long journey when the battery has died on my phone.

Synwire USB Cable and plug: Again, mainly used as an emergency power supply. Finally, the last item of tech that's is often in my pocket or bag is my YOSH waterproof case for my phone[29]. Again, very simple bit of tech that keeps my phone dry in extreme weather and I've even used it take some great under-water pictures in the sea.

---

[28] Nello Bike Bell. *https://www.palomarweb.com/product/nello/*

[29] YOSH Waterproof phone case. *http://www.yoshforyouth.com/show_17.html*

@ActivateLearn   Helen Blunden

Modern Workplace Learning Practitioner who loves to Work Out Loud! Creator; Blogger; Vlogger; Dot Connector with Quirks. Has been known to knit QR codes. Melbourne, Australia

Wearables

Glasses: Back in 1984 I was a young student in high school. I was that nerdy kid, always sitting up in front of the classroom closest to the blackboard and asking the teacher questions. At the time, I kidded myself that I was interested in my studies. In fact, I couldn't see the writing on the board. Only when I snatched the glasses off my friend's head one day and put them on, did I realise something was wrong with my eyesight.

That prank quietened me. I looked around the classroom and the world had burst in front of my eyes with all its glorious sharp colour. So THIS was how I was meant to see! I could see leaves on the trees and the titles on the spines of books on the shelves. Since then my myopia has been steadily deteriorating, however, it has slowed with age. As my friends and family urged me to have eye surgery to correct it, in all honesty, the only time my short sightedness became an issue was the deflated feeling when I put on a pair of virtual reality glasses and the entire effect was lost on me because I couldn't see anything. Nothing's as pathetic looking as someone donning a pair of VR glasses and looking around aimlessly with no reaction.

Watch: I've always been a stickler for time. I hate being late to anything and luckily my husband shares the same feeling. In our household, we have clocks in nearly every room that run five minutes early. This trait helped me well when I served in the Royal Australian Navy. Not only was I the first one to turn up at various meetings and events but I was mortified if I kept anyone waiting because I thought it was rude and impolite to discount someone else's time. Today, I wear a lovely Mickey Mouse watch that my husband bought for me when we were at Disney World in Florida because it reminded me of the first watch my father bought me when I was a little girl. As I work from home, I now wear the watch infrequently. I have more time on my hands and don't pay much attention to it. It's been quite liberating without it.

That's it for wearables. I used to wear the FitBit until I realised that I hated to be tethered with needless gadgets tracking my every movement and making me feel guilty. When I caught myself jogging on the spot at the end of my bed late one night because I hadn't completed my 10,000 steps in that day, I realised that I was its slave. I ditched it there and then and resolved that only I was responsible for my fitness. I had to change my own mindset and not have this gadget nag me to do it.

In my Pocket

As a female, there is nothing in my pockets. In fact, on the rare occasions that my clothes do have pockets, the only thing that goes in them are my hands if it's an exceptionally cold day and I need to keep them warm. After all, darling, it's the silhouette and the drape of our attire that we need to consider.

In my Bag

Purse: Someone once told me that it is bad luck to be given a purse for a gift and as such I banned my husband from ever buying me one for fear it might curse our marriage. My fear may be unjustified of course but when my mum handed me hers, I accepted it. It's a disgusting colour of baby poo brown and I figured that something so ugly already has had its fair share of bad luck. Invariably, the purse is nearly always empty except for some gold coins, seven library cards, one credit card and a plastic supermarket trolley token. I keep every single receipt and clean it out every few months. Someone once joked that every time I open my purse, moths fly out of it because it doesn't see the light of day. That part is true; I have an aversion to spending money. However, you can never have enough yarn. That's what I prefer to spend my money on.

iPhone: For many years, I had an iPhone 4 which served me well. In the last year, I upgraded to an iPhone 6 and I'm glad I did. I love the phone and all its functions. I do everything on this phone. I take photos and videos, play my music, use social media, read and respond to emails, access documents on Google Drive; have my airline tickets and even make actual phone calls (who would have thought!). I use it every single day. A few years back I bought a Samsung Galaxy Tablet 10" thinking that this would be my main tool but that lays discarded on a bedside table. I should have spent more time thinking about that purchase because it could have saved me a bit of money to spend on some nice angora yarn. How could I not have seen that the main device will always be the one that is most portable?

Back Up Charger: A vendor was giving these out at a conference and I raced up to grab one. It's been a lifesaver many times. I always had this strange fear of being kidnapped by some Hannibal Lecter character who puts you into a pit and you look down at your phone to call for help and see there's no charge left! Stuff of nightmares! So, there's comfort knowing that your phone is quietly being recharged in your hand bag and you don't need to hang around a power outlet late at night. If you're ever in a pit with Lecter peering in, you can be assured you'll have some charge left. Of course, you may not have mobile coverage but let's not quibble over trivialities.

Business Card Holder: Technically not a gadget but I got one after I realised that using apps to scan business cards or changing your business card into a QR code and asking people to scan it at conferences and events, resulted in them looking at you like the village idiot. I found out the hard way that business people are not ready for any electronic or technologically advanced way to share business cards through apps tapping phones together. They still rely on the physical process of handing over paper business cards. I had to go out and buy a pack of business cards and a holder.

Book: In the last couple of years, I have been taking a book with me to read when I have time in between appointments. That is, a physical book. Before then, I carried around the original Amazon Kindle which was a gift to me from my husband. On the Kindle, I download non-fiction books and have a wonderful collection (yes, I use the annotations and highlights and then use Amazon Kindle Notes to organise these notes into Evernote folders for each book). I'm an avid reader of nonfiction more than fiction but at times when I need a bit of escapism, I'm more likely to order the book from the library and read the physical book because I love the tactile nature of the pages and its smell. I've rediscovered the joy of the library and many of the business books there have been ordered on my recommendations.

Five Essential Apps

SMS: Technically not an app but a function I use daily on the phone. There's no two ways about it, the plan that we're on, texting between phones on similar data plans is quicker and cheaper. Until Australia can pretty much have Wi-Fi freely available everywhere, this will have to do.

Gmail: Some people say that email is on its way out. I'm not one of them. It'll be around for a long while yet. This is the second most used app on the phone where I check daily.

Safari: It's the browser of choice on my iPhone and used daily to look up things I need answers quickly.

Twitter: The Twitter iOS app is the most used social media app on my phone.

Maps: I use this app when I need to travel around town or drive to places I haven't been. I like to turn Siri on and hear my loud Greek parents exclaim in surprise and yell out in shock when they hear a stranger's voice on the phone. "Helen, someone is trying to talk to you!" Yes, it's Siri, she's directing us to our destination. "What? How does she know where we're going? Who is this woman? Is she Greek?" And so it goes on...

So, there you have it. Despite being an avid fan of technology and apps, many of which I use at my desk on a PC, when I'm out and about, my needs are relatively simple and old fashioned. Really, so long as I have my iPhone I can do without everything else including the actual bag to carry it all in. That's when I wish my clothes had an iPhone sized pocket.

@courosa   Alec Couros

Professor of educational technology and media at the University of Regina, Canada.

I was asked to describe the tech tools that I use on a daily basis: the tools I can't go without, the tools I "turn around and go back home to get." As I considered what to write, however, I realized that my favourite tools aren't just things I carry around with me in my bag - they have become integral to my daily functioning as part of the connected reality I live in. You might say I'm a bit of a cyborg in that sense, to use Haraway's language: she argues that "Technology is not neutral. We're inside of what we make, and it's inside of us." So, to give you a better sense of the technology that is integral to my work and leisure, I've chosen to describe a day in my augmented life.

The first thing I do each morning is to check the major news networks to see the state of the world. My go-to sources include CBC, CNN, and BBC. I will likely also spend a few minutes catching up on some of the nightly news shows, things like the Daily Show with Trevor Noah, the Late Show with Stephen Colbert, and Late Night with Seth Meyers. Perhaps not surprisingly, I do none of this via television, and if it weren't for the preference of my family, I'd declare myself a cord-cutter as I have little use for cable television services and prefer to ingest news on my own time.

Once I've determined that the world is more or less okay (at least, as okay as it's going to get in the Trump era), then I move on to personal communication. I use a range of platforms for this. First up is Twitter.

For me, Twitter is a professional platform for the most part, so here I will often find DMs and mentions from the educators all around the world who make up my personal learning network. I use Hootsuite to access Twitter from my phone, which allows me to easily check out a variety of hashtags, including those related to general education (*#edchat*), educational technology (*#edchat*), my various courses (*#ecmp355*, *#eci831*, etc.) and my local provincial politics (*#skpoli*).

Next stop is Facebook. That space has evolved much more into a place for family and friends, but I also get messages daily from victims who have been scammed by catfishers[30] who are using my photos (but that's fodder for a whole other chapter). Finally, it's on to my two email accounts, both of which I use for professional as well as personal reasons, but because of technical compatibilities I've never been able to consolidate the two.

Most of this morning communication is done on my phone (the new iPhone 7), which allows me to accomplish all of this while still in bed. Once I get to work, however, I prefer to use my big-screen desktop Mac, ideally with a secondary

---

[30] Definition: Catfish - *http://www.urbandictionary.com/define.php?term=catfish*

display monitor to give me maximum screen area. My daily routine at work includes many of the same platforms as well as additional ones. Central to my organization is my Chrome browser, which is personalized with extensions and bookmarks. Google Drive is another tool I'd be lost without. All of the material for my courses is there in nicely organized folders, and the real time shared editing capabilities make Google Docs my go-to choice for collaborations of every kind. One other key tool is my Digg Reader[31], where I can read the aggregated feeds of the few educational blogger voices who survived the great web 2.0 wars of the early 21st century (when Facebook and Twitter first emerged and drastically changed the distributed nature of the edublogosphere). Years after its untimely demise, I'm still mourning the loss of Google Reader. I feel this painfully at times when an instinct deep in my muscle memory manages to hijack my cognitive processes and I find found that I've typed Reader's URL in the address bar only to find the ruins of a forgotten time on the social web. Digg Reader is far from a perfect replacement of Google Reader, but it's the best replacement I've come across thus far.

While my preference is to work on big screens, I travel pretty extensively for work and so I have had to develop an on-the-road system as well. Central to my portable workstation is my laptop (a 13 inch Macbook Air that's a few years old but works fine, except that the hyphen key is really stubborn). To give me more screen space, I will often use my iPad as a secondary display using the Duet app[32]; this is especially helpful when I teach my online courses (typically using Zoom.us) while on the road. My iPhone is also a key piece of my travel gear: I use it for SMS, iMessage, and Facetime with family and friends, to check in on Swarm at whatever airport I happen to find myself in, or even to catch a Pokemon or two. Rounding out my travel must-haves are my Bose Quiet Comfort 35 headphones; not only do these provide fantastic noise cancellation (a blessing on airplanes or other forms of transit), but they also allow me to catch up on downloaded videos from great YouTube channels like Blog Brothers, Numberphile, Veritasium, VSauce, or Crash Course, to enjoy some documentaries on Netflix, or to reconnect to the angst of my youth by blasting a little hip hop or punk rock.

And finally, I suppose I should mention the bedrock upon which almost all my daily activities rest: access to the internet. I'm not ashamed to say that I've adopted a connectionist view of life: that is, that we can be persistently connected and still live a balanced life. If I could produce my own Wi-Fi I would, but for now I rely on the commercially available variety, including my Gogo Inflight Internet account, which satisfies my need for connectivity (although somewhat sluggish) even at thirty thousand feet.

So, there you have it: a rundown of the tech I use daily as part of my connected, augmented - and maybe even a little cyborgian - life.

---

[31] Digg Reader - *http://digg.com/reader*

[32] Duet iOS app - *https://www.duetdisplay.com/*

@samillingworth   **Sam Illiningworth**

Senior lecturer in Science Communication with an unhealthy love of satellites and Japanese RPGs. Fine purveyor of bad poetry. Manchester, UK

In my current role, I am rarely sat down at my desk for any prolonged period of time. As such, I had a think about what items are absolutely essential for me to be able to do my job effectively. This is what I came up with.

Wearables
Glasses: The analogue variety, without which I would not be able to accomplish very much at all. I am short sighted with a mild myopia, which means that I'm all in for a magnification of -7 in both eyes. For those of you who are not au fait with the nomenclature of opticians, this is extremely short sighted, and without my glasses I can barely make out the details of a hand in front of my face, let alone a digital screen. I often wear contact lenses as well, but I find that staring at a computer monitor for large parts of the day means that my eyes often dry out, and so I always have my glasses on standby, just in case. They are now a part of my identity, and the only time that I really begrudge them is when I go swimming, or when I get up in the middle of the night to check that I have locked the front door.

Watch: As you can probably tell from my antics with the front door, I am definitely on the OCD spectrum, and nowhere is this more evident than in my relation to time keeping. I HATE being even a minute late for anything, and if I am meeting someone in a new location I will either turn up ridiculously (read 30-40 minutes) early or else conduct a recce beforehand. I am constantly checking the time, which I know must appear incredibly rude to whoever I am speaking to, but I promise that it is not because I am bored, it is just because... well I'm not sure why I do it, but please do not be offended if you see me anxiously checking my watch in a meeting. For years I wore a series of sports watches and cheap Casio models, but recently I decided that the Omega watch that my Nana bought me for my 21st birthday was gathering dust in a cupboard somewhere, and that nice things shouldn't just be saved just for special occasions...

In my Pockets
Wallet: My wallet currently seems to have the density of a neutron star. I blame two things for this: my Yorkshire heritage and my love of caffeine. The latter meaning that I regularly frequent a bevy of coffee shops, and the former meaning that I absolutely must collect a discount card for every shop that I go into, even if it is an independent tearoom in a small Buckinghamshire hamlet that I have no intention of revisiting. These cards are of course fastidiously organised and categorised within the confines of my wallet, which itself has seen better days, but which I am loathe to update as I find it's fraying leather somewhat comforting.

iPhone: I currently have an iPhone 6, and it is without a doubt the most useful piece of kit in my digital arsenal. Whereas there would have been a time when I absolutely refused to leave the house without my wallet, this is no longer the case, with Apple Pay having helped to revolutionise my consumer experience. Similarly, coffee shop loyalty apps mean that the density of my wallet is slowly diminishing.

Being constantly on the move, the ability to respond to email and monitor my social media accounts at any time is extremely useful, and I would say that I could do almost all aspects of my job using just my mobile phone. In fact, the only time I find it frustrating is when writing and editing documents, as I am yet to find an application that allows me to write with the same ease as on a laptop. However, once someone comes up with a word-processing app that is designed specifically for the iOS, then I will be able to go fully mobile. To all those non-Apple fans out there, I did try using a Windows phone once, but I found it to be so counter-intuitive that I soon lost patience and reverted to type, sorry.

Five Essential Apps

Dropbox: The Ability to see and read all my documents at anytime, anywhere there is a decent Wi-Fi or mobile data signal is wonderful. However, probably the most useful feature is the ability to instantly email a link for a document to a someone whilst I am talking to them, thereby saving me the hassle of forgetting to do it when I get back to the office.

Twitter: Others will disagree, but I find the official Twitter app to be an easy-to-use and well-designed portal.

WhatsApp: Being able to connect with my family and friends at any time, and for free, no matter where we are in the world is a luxury that I absolutely take for granted. I also find that it helps to let off steam in relation to major world events on private WhatsApp message groups before posting more considered responses on public social media accounts.

National Rail: The British train system being as unreliable as it is, this app is essential, as it allows me to plan my daily commute to the nearest minute. Thereby helping me to avoid waiting around on crowded platforms for severely delayed trains, when instead I could still be in bed.

TripAdvisor: Why bother finding out for yourself if a café or hotel is any good, when you can rely on the opinions of millions of others to help do it for you? Whilst individual reviews often need to be taken with a pinch of salt, this app has saved me time, money and stomach cramps on numerous occasions, both home and abroad.

In my Bag

MacBook Pro: I've been using a MacBook for the best part of the last decade now, and after switching from a Windows-based machine I can't see myself going back anytime soon. I know that IT purists might disagree, and I apologise if (like most Apple users) I come across as a little bit 'salesy,' but I just find them an absolute joy to use. My current model is a MacBook Pro (Retina, 13-inch, late

2013 model), and I use it both at home and in the office, where I hook it up to a 27" Thunderbolt display, along with an Apple keyboard and a non-Apple mouse. For whilst I might be an Apple acolyte, there is nothing on this Earth that can convince me that the Apple mouse is useful as anything other than an over-priced paperweight.

Kindle: Recently I got rid of my large CD and DVD collections, figuring that I would be better served by streaming services such as Spotify and Netflix instead, and whilst I am sure that this will cause many of you to break out in cold sweats, it has definitely worked; enabling me to reclaim large areas of shelving throughout the house. For some unknown reason though I feel loathe to do the same thing with my books, as I find having shelves of reading material to be an oddly satisfying concept. Therefore, whilst I use my kindle regularly, for both pleasure and work-related literature, I doubt that I will ever be able to move my entire book collection over to the cloud. I think it might be something to do with the way that books smell, e-ink just isn't musty enough...

If I were to compile a list of items that were needed for me to be able to live my personal life effectively, then I think that it would be a fairly similar list. I hesitate in using the phrase 'could not live without' in relation to a piece of technology, as I think that it should be reserved for lovers, music and poetry, but I really would struggle without my iPhone. Or at least I would to begin with; after a while I suspect that I might even begin to warm to the idea of not checking for emails every thirty seconds...

@NomadWarMachine   Sarah Honeychurch

Philosopher, Doctor Who geek, knitter, uke player. Learning Tech *@UofGlasgow*; Editor *@HybridPed*. *#jisc50social*. Glasgow, UK

I never thought of myself as a geek - as a child I was always knitting, sewing and reading and was under-impressed by the computers my dad and brother pored over. But I've ended up working as a Learning Technologist and married to a software engineer, and I have a lot of gadgets now.

In my bag

I am rarely without my sensible black, multi-sectioned handbag. As well as the usual keys, money and cards, I cram in my Nexus 7 android tablet, a Kindle Touch loaded with trashy crime fiction as well as serious tomes such as Vygotsky and Deleuze and Guattari, and Archos MP3 player and earbuds that I forget about most of the time, my Canon SX280 (I adore this camera - it is so easy to point and click and it makes me look like a decent photographer), and whichever pair of socks are on my knitting needles at the moment. My Motorola android phone will be in my bag if I am not using it or charging it. I also have two Anker portable chargers, and one of those will always be in my bag. Sometimes I also pick up my Zoom audio recorder - great for recording the sounds of my city and sharing them with my cMOOC pals. Then, of course, I carry way too many pens - I like Stabilo point 88 and always have at least three with me (black, pink and purple) as well as a highlighter and a retractable pencil. I also have a watch in my bag that I will wear when I'm teaching or if I'm away from a computer.

If I'm travelling, I'll have my Dell laptop with me – my husband told me that I wanted this when he bought himself one and he was absolutely right - it's so light that I can hold it in one hand, but it is fast and has a decent sized screen; and an Anker multi-point charger along with various cables. And, of course, I always pack spare yarn and needles when I'm away - train journeys are perfect for whipping through my stash. Finally, when I remember, I'll also load my Kindle Fire with films and take that away with me - I don't watch many films, but I do like curling up in a hotel bed and watching some pure trash.

On my phone/tablet

As these are both android, my phone and Nexus sync with each other, so most of the time I'll download a new app to both. Obviously, I have Facebook and Twitter as apps, though when I'm at my PC I'll use Tweetdeck instead of Twitter so that I can quickly see what's going on in #CLMooc, #DigPed and #DS106. I also use Slack through the app on my phone and tablet - we use it at Hybrid Pedagogy to keep track of who is editing what, and we used it to organise #CLMooc this summer. Gmail pushes notifications to my mobile tech (I have a personal Gmail account as well as a Hybrid Pedagogy one); my work email is setup on my phone, but on my tablet I just access it through the web interface.

Chrome is my default browser, (though I will switch to Firefox if I am using Zotero on my desktop, as it just works better for that). I use Pocket a lot to save web pages to read later - especially when I am flicking through tweets on my phone - it's often easier for me to read things on a larger screen later. I also use Evernote as well, but have stopped using it - I am not sure why. Likewise, InoReader[33] - I'd forgotten about having that until I flicked through my mobile apps to write about my *#EdTechRations*.

I use Facebook Messenger on my tablet but not on my phone - if I need to access it when I am away from any Wi-Fi then I'll use my phone as a hotspot and use my tablet to read the message. I do prefer to chat via Twitter DM, nowadays. I also have the Trainline app on both devices - useful recently to be able to use this on my phone while Glasgow Queen Street was being refurbished and the trains were not at their regular times. I use Google Maps a lot as well when I'm away on business - I have no sense of direction and use it to orient myself before trying to find a new hotel or venue.

I do have Google Drive on both phone and tablet, but really dislike using the mobile interface to edit - when I'm doing some collaborative authoring (as I often am) I'll tend to look at comments on my mobile tech then switch to a laptop/PC if I need to edit or comment. This means that I rarely do any collaborative authoring after 8pm, which I think is a good thing.

I mainly read books on my Kindle, but if it is being charged (I forget that this needs to be done fairly regularly), it syncs to the app on my phone and tablet, which is useful - especially if I discover on the train that my Kindle is out of charge again.

So that's it - if pushed I could manage with just my phone most of the time, but I do like the extra functionality of my other gadgets.

---

[33] Inoreader - *http://www.inoreader.com/*

@josepicardoSHS   José Picardo

Assistant Principal @*SurbitonHigh* - Interested in pedagogy, digital strategy and the provision of a broad, well-rounded education. London, UK

Given my manifest interest in educational technology, folks often expect me to own lots of gadgets and to be always up-to-date with the latest smartphone, laptop or what have you. Or perhaps they assume I'm forever 'staring into' a screen. In reality, I am the humble owner a single smartphone and that's about it. I do use a laptop and also a tablet for work, but these are provided by my employer – though I do bring them home almost always. Whether owned by me or by my employer, below is a little run down of the technology I rely on most frequently:

Wearables
I generally avoid wearables. I am not philosophically opposed to them, I just find that electronic devices can, if their use is left unmonitored, reverse the roles and become our masters, rather than the other way around.

For this reason, the only technology I wear – aside from a wedding band and a leather bracelet that my children presented to me – is my glasses or contact lenses that I use to correct the myopia I developed partly due to some suspect genes and partly due to 'staring into' books lots during childhood.

I wear no watch – smart or otherwise – nor do I use fitness trackers. If I need to know the time, and depending on where I am, I just check my smartphone, my laptop's taskbar or look up at the radio-controlled clock in my classroom.

In my pockets
My clothes have pockets. These allow me to carry a variety of useful tools that allow me to do the things I consider normal in my life. The contents of my pockets are constantly changing, but there are three items that are ever present:

Keyring: On it hang a variety of keys and electronic fobs that allow me entry to my home, car, office and the classrooms where I teach.

Wallet: As well as few coins and the occasional ten-pound note, my wallet stores a selection of contactless smart cards that allow me to travel and shop without having to carry cash with me. Even though I love my brown leather wallet and its understated elegance, I look forward to the day when technology allows me to travel and shop even without it and the cards it carries.

Smartphone: It's an iPhone 6S Plus. It's not too big, despite what you might think. It's perfect. Since I hardly ever make or receive phone calls on it, its size is ideal to carry around in my pockets and communicate with others – via email or social media – or comfortably read books, magazines and newspapers on the go. I even use it to regulate my central heating! I also take most of my photos using it, which are of excellent quality, so I don't need a separate compact camera. I also use my smartphone as a portable music player, so I don't own a separate one of those either.

In my briefcase/bag
An elegant tan leather satchel-style briefcase allows me to carry the tools of my trade in comfort. Its contents vary depending on the day or occasion, but the things you will always find there are:

Laptop: My three-year-old MacBook Air 13 inch is the perfect laptop as far as I am concerned. It's thin, it's light, it's powerful and it simply will not run out of juice, even after being put through its paces all day planning lessons, writing or editing media. This means that I don't have to carry a cable charger with me. Laptop range anxiety is thankfully a thing of the past.

Tablet: My iPad Pro 9 inch is a simply fantastic multipurpose device that I use constantly as my teacher planner, calendar and notebook. With it I read, write, watch, listen and generally learn stuff. It's my portable interactive whiteboard, camera, e-book reader (thank heavens for the Kindle app) and general repository of teaching and learning resources.

Bits of paper: Exercise books, textbooks, crumpled half-marked essays, post-it notes whose stickiness has long been emasculated by dust and fluff and numerous receipts printed on creased thermal paper faded by the passing of time and forgetfulness to fill in the requisite expenses form. Though I recognise I use less of it these days, I love paper. It's still the best tool for the job on many occasions. Long may it last.

Green pens: Yes, I mark using green. Bite me!

At home
The combination of reliable fast broadband and an Apple TV means that TV watching is more and more an a-la-carte affair. My children don't remember a world before on-demand TV and to them the confines and limitations of scheduled live TV are as quaint as recording your music on shiny silver discs.

In terms of future tech, I can't wait to get rid of my smoke-belching, diesel-chugging dad-taxi and replace it with a nice, clean hybrid or fully electric car. That's what middle class does to you.

As a keen but rather average photographer, I also own a Canon DSLR camera that I take on holidays, day trips and walks. It does only one job and it's excellent at it. There's much to be said for that.

@CosmicCork   **Cormac Cahill**

Primary Teacher, Apple Distinguished Educator, Apple Education Trainer, Book Creator Ambassador, Passionate advocate of technology in the classroom, Optimist. Cork, Ireland

For a long time, the technology I carried was minimal, simply because I just couldn't afford much of it. But as the years have gone by I find that I have learned to actually save towards something I want. I am not somebody who queues up outside a store waiting to be the first to have something. I generally like to wait, see what all the fuss is about and then decide if I want something. As a result, I tend to have very little technology that I don't use. What I buy I find multiple uses for. Most of this tech is bought from my trusty piggy bank. I empty my pocket of coins at the end of the day and when the bank is full I buy a gadget of some description. I may have to re-think this strategy though as these days I seem to have less coins in my pocket as everything is paid for by card.

A rucksack is my carrier of choice. I find it easier to carry everything around on my back than having it by my side. I bought one with multiple pockets and everything has its place. In the rucksack you will find;

Laptop: It seems to go everywhere with me, even when I am not using it. I went for a Mac Pro rather than an Air as I live in the countryside of Ireland and the broadband speeds here are pretty horrific. Put quite simply I cannot rely on The Cloud. I need to have access to everything without the need to connect to the internet. The hard drive is 1TB and it is almost full. I regularly have to spend a little time deleting or moving projects to one of a number of backup drives I have (which I also carry around). Sad to say but I get a kick out of suddenly clearing up another 100GB of space for myself from time to time.

Tablet: I make less use of this now than I used to but working in a school means it is always with me. I have two iPads and the kids in the classroom basically own them. I don't have them filled with apps but keep just a few that the kids make incredible use of. Book Creator for creating books and comics, iMovie for making incredible movies and Minecraft to get the creative juices flowing. I am toying with the idea of upgrading to the iPad Pro especially as it's now available in the smaller size.

Phone: My iPhone 6. This is probably the one I use the most. It is rarely used as an actual phone but it does contain my music for listening to in the car as I commute to work, games to keep me occupied when I am waiting somewhere and apps such as Facebook and Twitter for keeping in touch. I went for the 64GB one as I am constantly taking photographs and videos. Most of these are also edited on the iPhone as the range of editing apps available is incredible.

Apple Watch: You may be noticing a certain trend here. I am a fan of Apple technologies. The fact that they all work so seamlessly together just makes things easier. The Watch is the latest edition and while I don't really use it for keeping track of fitness, etc. I do love the ease with which I can receive texts, tweets and other notifications.

Battery Charger: Because of all of this technology I naturally have to carry a battery charger with me. I can't remember where I picked it up and I can't even see a logo on it but it helps top up my many devices when needed. I also like to go camping and naturally I have to carry all of this tech with me so I also have a bigger one in the camper van to keep everything running smoothly.

Adaptors and Cables: In the rucksack you will also find a VGA to 30 pin connector, a VGA to lightning connector, a VGA connector for my Mac (used especially in school and at various workshops and conferences) and a variety of charging cables.

Rocketbook Wave: This was my latest purchase after spotting it on Kickstarter. It's basically the only notebook I will ever need. I write on the page (I do carry a pen) and use my phone to scan the page where it is automatically uploaded to Dropbox, Google Drive or iCloud. When the notebook is filled I pop it in the microwave for a few minutes and all the pages are wiped clean allowing me to start using it all over again. It's been wonderful in my attempt to go paperless[34].

iPod and headphones: From to time my iPod gets thrown in when I need to have more space on my phone and I still need to carry my music with me wherever I go. Headphones too are thrown in the bag. Nothing too fancy here. Just the standard iPhone headphones are used. I find some of the newer varieties far too bulky.

Shoulderpod and microphone: I got a Shoulderpod[35] last year so that I could attach my phone to a tripod but it's also made filming while holding the phone so much better. I also recently added a Rode microphone[36] which has been great to use. I regret not forking out though for the one with the built in battery as I have noticed it does help drain the iPhone battery quickly.

GoPro: I carry a GoPro with me when I am on my holidays. It's sometimes attached to the front of my camper van or bike to get those shots that I would rather not use my iPhone to get.

Having just looked back over the list I know now why I have a rucksack. I'm almost afraid to think what this weighs but the rucksack makes transporting it all a breeze!

---

[34] Rocketbook Wave: *http://getrocketbook.com/*

[35] Shoulderpod: *http://www.shoulderpod.com/*

[36] Rode VideoMic Go: *http://www.rode.com/microphones/videomicgo*

@catspyjamasnz   **Joyce Seitzinger**

Education technologist & networked learner. Learner experience design *@lxdesignco*. Badges. Network practice in edu & research. Founder *@academictribe*. Melbourne, Australia

Over the last three years I have actively been shifting my role from 'EdTech' to a learning experience designer. In 2014 I nearly left the industry all together. I was getting increasingly disillusioned with how many of the projects I worked on seemed not all that different from projects I had worked on 10 years earlier. Despite some of the amazing digital experiences that were being created in other industries, with the exception of the occasional groundbreaking pilot, so much of the work I did was still around setting up course shells to support a very low-end, functional version of blended learning. Seeing the excitement and possibility elsewhere I thought that maybe it was time to turn a corner, and so I started to hang out in Melbourne's super active startup scene. Pretty soon I encountered a new tribe of people called experience designers; some were UX specialists, some worked in service design, but they were all focused on creating amazing experiences for their 'users'. How they went about their work fascinated me and I could see how their methods might work for learning design too. After all aren't we all trying to create amazing digital learning experiences for our learners?

So, for the last three years through General Assembly workshops, participating in hackathons, reading what I can and sheer trial and error, I've tried to cocoon myself and become a new hybrid creature: a 'learning experience designer'. From this we are also pivoting Academic Tribe to be more focused on LX Design.

As I've upskilled the biggest realisation I've had is that, as an experience designer, you really don't do much of the design yourself. Your role is to facilitate the design process, so that everyone involved in the project can contribute from their own expertise and so jointly design for experience.

So, this is where my main *#EdTechRation* comes in. **Post-its.** You can't help a diverse team of experts to co-design a learning solution, when all their assumptions, ideas, thinking and expertise is locked up in their heads and only emerging through slow, threaded conversation. Post-it notes might seem simple, but they are the key to unlocking, uncovering and unpacking, the solution that is hidden in your design team's collective heads.

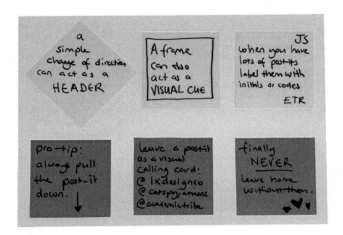

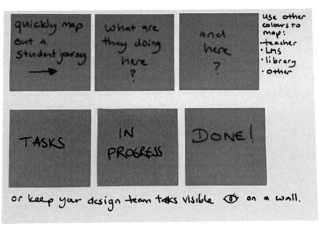

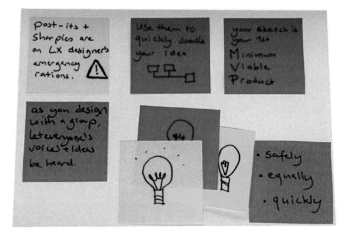

In my bag

First of all, I changed my bag in the last few weeks. Working as a consultant I can find myself quite itinerant among the gorgeous buildings of Melbourne's universities. As a result, I ended up carrying a little "mobile office' in my bright pink Fossil handbag. Two weeks ago, I exchanged this for a nice stylish Evecase grey versatile backpack / shoulder bag. As much as I loved the fact that my tiny MacBook Air could fit into my feminine pretty handbag, I had to face facts and admit that both my shoulders and the handles were feeling the pain, as I increasingly carried notebooks, pens, post-its, bluetack and more. A few years ago, when we moved, we KonMari'd[37] our house and, from that, I learned to be quite ruthless when tempted to hang on to things that I 'might someday need' or things that were kept around out of habit. I also learned to accept the objects I do need and arrange them so I can easily find and use them. I applied this to my office, but it's taken me until the last few weeks to finally accept that goes for my mobile office, bag plus contents, too. So, what's made the cut?

- 2 Notebooks (1 with per-week view for planning/reflection, 1 for hefty note taking and sketching)
- Pencil case (Pencils, stylus, USB sticks, VGA connectors, markers, sharpies)
- 3-4 Sharpies
- 2 or 3 little stacks of Post-its
- Bluetack
- MacBook Air
- Charger
- Power bar (my iPhone battery has issues)
- iPad
- iPhone
- iPhone charger
- Make-up bag
- Wallet
- Noise-cancelling earbuds. I've invested in the Bose ones. Expensive but indispensable when trying to find good 'mobile office' spots in often busy cafes or shared workspaces.

On my phone/iPad

My phone and iPad have become my 'on-the-go' devices and the home screens have been set up for business. Most important apps?

- When brainstorming, and sketching for design purposes, the resulting artefacts can be meaningless to people who weren't in the room. But for the participants the visuals can acts as triggers to recall the shared understanding that grew. So, during and after sessions I will snap away and then afterwards share the pictures via Google Drive.
- Slack for communicating with the distributed Academic Tribe team and

[37] Maria Kondo and the KonMari method - *https://en.wikipedia.org/wiki/Marie_Kondo*

increasingly client project teams

- Asana[38] and Trello for task management. Different clients use different productivity software, so task management can sometimes be a bit of a nightmare.
- Gmail. I really don't like email preferring messaging platforms like Slack or Hangouts for chatting to people I'm working with. But it is a necessary evil for any business.
- Google Drive and Dropbox for having access to all the files I need on the go.
- Twitter so I can keep in touch and learn from all my smart EdTech and design colleagues.
- Casts - I love, love, love podcasts. Can't get enough of them. I follow many UX and Design podcasts so I can keep learning in my new field.
- Not on the home screen of my iPhone, the Phone app. I rarely call people on the phone and I really don't like getting phone calls either. Yep, don't call me maybe. And I positively detest voicemails. Impromptu phone calls and voicemails just feel so inefficient, I can't see you, we can't share artefacts, you and I can't connect. I would much rather send or receive texts and then set up a Skype or Google Hangout where documents or work-in-progress can be shared and we can really get work.

---

[38] Asana - *https://asana.com/*

@HeyWayne   **Wayne Barry**

Learning Technologist #CCCU | PGCAP Tutor | #EdD Candidate | CTA #edcMOOC | #Blogger | #Genealogist | #Cartophilist | #Cinephile. Canterbury, UK

I have been a Learning Technologist since 2006, and have been fortunate and privileged enough to attend a myriad of interesting (and not-so-interesting) conferences and symposiums. It always amuses me when I see people carrying heavy-looking rucksacks or bags around conference halls which are fit to burst at the seams with an excess of technological gadgetry and widgetry.

Personally, I like to travel light; a bit like that chap MacGyver, who was always resourceful and relied upon his wits and a Swiss Army knife. My technology needs are minimalistic and ascetic. For everything else, I rely on my wits, resilience and imagination.

Assistive Technologies
These are bits of 'kit' that I cannot live without - they form part of my identity. Life, work and learning are quite literally stalled and prohibited without them.

Glasses: I am short-sighted, so without them, I cannot read, drive or study peoples' faces. I use a lot of technology that is dependent upon my eyesight: smartphones, tablets, laptops, desktop computers and cameras. All these tools would not be so easily accessible to me.

Hearing Aids: I have a hearing impairment in both ears. I have a job that involves talking and, more importantly, listening to people. I have to present and communicate ideas, advice and information. I need to be able to respond effectively to any questions that are asked of me. Without my hearing aids, this particular world would be shut off from me.

Wristwatch: I have a Seiko Kinetic Perpetual wristwatch that combines the classic beauty of a mechanical watch with all of the advantages of kinetic technology; it is powered by the movement of my body. No winding up. No battery changes. I border on having OCD, but my day is very much structured around the rhythm of time. Always a bit early, but never too late.

Containment Technologies
I really LOVE bags that are teeming with pockets and zipped compartments. They need to be light to carry and compact enough to carry my 'emergency rations'.

Messenger Bag: A big, green bag from Fossil that I take to work with me. It has lots of pockets and compartments for storing all of my essential technology for work, such as Samsung Galaxy S6 Edge Smartphone, Apple iPad Mini with Logitech Ultrathin Keyboard Cover[39], Tweed pencil case (with pens, pencils and highlighters), notepads, University business cards, Staff ID card, USB sticks, Victorinox Swiss Card[40] (Oh yes! I have a Swiss Army knife), Kensington Wireless USB presenter with red laser pointer, and, of course, my lunch box.

Slim Case: A recent acquisition for conferences and is manufactured by Gino Ferrari[41]. Again, there are loads of zipped compartments for the Samsung smartphone, iPad mini, pens, notepads, business cards, Moo MiniCards[42], USB sticks, Victorinox Swiss Card, and the wireless USB presenter.

That's not all, there are pockets for my passport, Canon PowerShot SX100 IS camera, Veho Pebble Verto Pro Portable Battery Charger[43], a mini LED flashlight torch, a Go Travel Micro Fan, and some spare batteries. It is all, surprisingly, very light to carry.

Shoulder Bag: My trusty old Troop Classic Canvas Shoulder Bag. It goes everywhere with me. There are spaces for my Samsung smartphone, Samsung Galaxy Note 8.0 tablet & stylus, pen, notepad, Victorinox Swiss Card, PowerShot camera, Pebble battery charger, mini LED flashlight torch, the Micro Fan, and some spare batteries. This, too, is very light to carry.

Essential Technologies

These are the 'must have' technologies that enables, sustains and supports me in becoming a critically reflective and evidence-informed professional and practitioner of technology enhanced learning.

Smartphone: I recently purchased the Samsung Galaxy S6 Edge smartphone. This piece of technology alone has become my 'Swiss Army Knife'. It keeps me informed and entertained. It allows me to communicate and collaborate. It has a camera and a flashlight. I can use it to record and collect evidence of good practice. I use Feedly for learning technology news, academic journal articles and blog posts from key thought leaders in our field. WhatsApp is used to maintain contact with friends, colleagues and my fellow doctoral candidates. Twitter allows me to maintain my professional learning networks.

Powerbank: You only need to attend one or two conferences to realise that you and everyone else and their dog are scrambling to sit next to the nearest available power socket. So, I invested in the Veho Pebble Verto Pro Portable Battery Charger with its assortment of connectors and cables, enabling my

---

[39] Logitech Ultrathin Keyboard Cover: *http://www.logitech.com/en-gb/product/ultrathin-keyboard-cover*

[40] Victorinox Swiss Card: *https://www.victorinox.com/uk/en/Products/Swiss-Army-Knives/SwissCards/c/SAK_SwissCard*

[41] Gino Ferrari: *https://ginoferrari.com/products/arke-16inch-laptop-slim-case*

[42] Moo mini cards: *https://www.moo.com/uk/products/minicards.html*

[43] Veho Pebble Vertoo Pro Portable Battery Charger: *http://www.veho-uk.com/main/shop_detail.aspx?article=289*

technology to function for a bit longer until I was able to properly charge it up. This has become the 'sharpener' to my 'Swiss Army Knife'.

Presentation Clicker: When presenting, I absolutely loathe being tethered to the keyboard or mouse of a computer. I like to wander around and pace up and down. I want to be and feel free. The Kensington Wireless USB presenter with its red laser pointer enables me to do just that

Camera: The camera allows me to explore and express my creative and artistic side. I bought the Canon PowerShot SX100 IS quite a few years ago to capture and curate memories and experiences. This tends to get used more when I am out and about.

Notepad and Pen: There must always be a 'Plan B' should the technology go into *#epicfail*. I always carry a notepad and pen with me. I like the tactile, kinesthetic feel where the paper, pen, hand and mind are as one. There is something immensely satisfying about watching ink take shape and form on paper. It is where ideas, stories, and lyrics are borne. It is where lists are made.

Water Bottle: No 'emergency ration' is complete without a bottle of water to freshen the body, rehydrate the "little grey cells", and to quench your thirst.

Specific Technologies

These technologies are used on an ad hoc basis, usually with a particular purpose or function in mind and can be introduced to my 'essential kit' at any time.

Tablet: Work provided me with an Apple iPad Mini with a Logitech Ultrathin Keyboard Cover. It enables me to keep up-to-date with my email and check my diary. It is used extensively to demonstrate bits of kit, like classroom response systems, such as Socrative or Plickers. In meetings, I use Evernote to make notes or access the mountain of papers that need to be read and digested. It effectively allows me to work on the move and be sustainable.

Audio Recorder: I purchased the Roland R-05 Wave/MP3 Recorder[44] with the Manfrotto PIXI Mini Tripod[45] as part of the data collection phase of my doctoral research. You get superb crisp sound quality that is 'music' to any transcriber's ears.

Music Player: If I am travelling or I need to unwind after a particularly vexing day, then my old Apple 16Gb iPod Touch gets a bit of an airing. This is the one device, along with the water bottle, that is crucial to my health and wellbeing. It is guaranteed to transport me mentally, spiritually and emotionally to somewhere far away from the stresses and strains of the real world.

---

[44] Roland R-05: *http://www.roland.co.uk/products/r-05/*

[45] Manfrotto PIXI Mini Tripod: *https://www.manfrotto.co.uk/pixi-mini-tripod-black*

@jsecker   **Jane Secker**

Copyright and Digital Literacy Advisor, LSE

My survival kit is based around the technology I use to do my research, writing, much of which is collaborative. I've decided to limit myself to 10 items as I think I could have written a very long list otherwise! They are in no particular order than the order they occurred to me!

1) **MacBook Air**. I discovered a love for Macs when I was about 13, when my Dad brought one home from work and I used it to design party invitations. I made some pretty terrible creations using clip art but it was easy to use. I didn't touch a Mac then for about 20 years and when I did I loved it all over again. It's neat and fits in my bag. It's light and I take it pretty much everywhere these days. The only bummer is it belongs to my employer technically and the battery life has deteriorated. I doubt I know how half of it works either, but it's a thing of beauty and we are inseparable.

2) **Wunderlist**[46]. Anyone who has met me in the last 3 years will know my conversion to the to-do list app Wunderlist. It's nothing fancy but it keeps me on track. I tried Trello, but it's Wunderlist that does it for me. I manage all my projects using it and the things I need to do out of work. I store notes in it and I have endless chats in the comments with my research partner as we use it to manage our various projects. Without Wunderlist I fear little would get done. I enjoy nothing more than looking at lists of things to do and ticking them off when they are done. The satisfying ping of the Wunderlist app, the way I have been able to customize it with a dreamy looking ginger cat, all adds to the wunder!

3) **Twitter**. I am a huge fan of Twitter. I joined it back in 2008 and there are very few days (apart from when I am on holiday) when I don't tweet. But it's become my way of finding out what's happening in the world. I read the news on Twitter first thing every morning. I use it to ping things of interest to colleagues. I remind myself to read things by favouriting them on Twitter. I follow people with similar interests and I get to participate in conferences and chats about issues I care about through following hashtags. For my professional development and keeping up to date I cannot think of a better place to spend time online!

4) **Dropbox**. Yes, I know there are issues, but I find Dropbox essential to my work these days and use it to store pretty much every file of importance. I can get to it pretty much anywhere, and the way I have it set up, provided I have my MacBook Air, that is pretty much everywhere. I can also collaborate with people, so it's a great way of working on a draft together. I know some people like Google Docs for the real time editing

---

[46] Wunderlist - *https://www.wunderlist.com/*

and the fact you never get conflict errors, but for me Dropbox just works. I even use it on my phone these days.

5) **WordPress.** I discovered WordPress back in 2007, when I decided to explore blogging. I set up a blog as part of a project about using social media in libraries. I started writing updates as blog post to let the project team know how it was progressing they told me they found it really useful. When that project finished, the blog morphed into my personal blog. WordPress is so easy to use; however, I also love the fact that you can do some really cool things with fairly minimal technical skills. I've taught others how to use WordPress and I now have multiple blogs that I contribute to, in addition to those used at LSE. It's a great way of creating a website so I used to host the information literacy research I produced with Emma Coonan back in 2011 on a WordPress blog and recently set up the Copyright Literacy website with Chris Morrison.

6) **Evernote.** This was one app I felt I could live without for quite some time, until one day at a conference when I started using it instead of word documents for my partly formed thoughts and notes. I have really started to find it difficult to live without Evernote and, when I attend a conference or meeting, I write my notes here. Anything important at some point gets turned into a Word document that ends up in Dropbox but for ideas and partly formed thoughts, Evernote is essential. Again, it's the collaborative features I like a lot; with the shared notebooks I can see what my co-researcher is up to, send them a quick note (as if I needed another communication platform!). The search feature is fabulous. I use it occasionally to clip content from the web, or to share a photo, but generally Evernote is like the paper notebooks which I still often with me.

7) **Slack.** I am a recent convert to Slack. There was me thinking I really didn't need another communication channel but I find it extremely helpful at cutting down on email traffic. I am a member of 4 Slack communities. We've started using it in the team I work in. I also am part of a Slack community for the copyright officers in London and one week into using it I can see how helpful it can be. I was really reluctant to use email for this group to communicate as no one needs more messages in their inbox. Slack is a great way of sharing something fairly trivial with people which really doesn't justify an email. Using the channels means people can filter what they are interested in and control how many or few notifications they want to get.

8) **WileyFox Phone**[47]. Thinking about all these apps I use I realized that the one device I am almost never without is my smartphone. Up until a year or so ago I had an iPhone, it seemed the way to go with having a Mac. However, I was getting increasingly fed up at how slow it was becoming,

---

[47] WileyFox Phone - *https://www.wileyfox.com/*

how little memory it had and how expensive the next upgrade was going to be. WileyFox was suggested to me by a tech guy I used to work with. He told me I would love it, and on a whim (I think it was an Amazon Black Friday) I ordered it. I haven't looked back going over to Android. Some of the features I particularly like are the integration with Google. The fact my photos appear like magic in Google Photos is great. But basically I just like the fact it's sleek, elegant, fast and effective.

9) **Creative Commons Licensed images.** In addition to taking my own photos for use online, one of the things I use a lot are openly licensed images. I say Creative Commons licensed images as that is what most of them are, and I generally use the Creative Commons Search to find images for my blogs and websites, or to use in PowerPoint slides. I recently discovered Unsplash[48], which has CC-0 images, meaning you don't even need to credit the photographer or artist. Because I spend my time teaching people about copyright and respect for others creativity, Creative Commons is a fantastic concept to introduce to staff, students and everyone. Yes, I know technically we can take images off the web, but I don't. I use images where people are happy to share them and give you a license to do this and give them credit!

10) **The internet.** I do wonder if I could do my job or manage my life without the internet. Obviously as someone born in the 1970s I can remember a time before the internet. I grew up only imagining a time when all the information I wanted might be available at the click of a button and spent hours pouring over books, visiting my local library and trying to make my Vic-20 computer do something interesting! But I've been on the internet in some form since about 1992 when I got my first email account (I had very few people to email in those days!) and, when I was studying for my PhD in the mid 1990s, I helped teach people how to use early browsers (Mosaic and Netscape Navigator) search engines (remembers Ask Jeeves?) and became familiar with telnet, ftp and Usenet news groups (although you didn't want to dig too deeply in them).

I love the internet, it's a wonderful invention, thank you Tim Berners-Lee. Yes, sometime we all need to be reminded that not everything is online, and that we need to apply the even more rigourous critical thinking to the information we find. We know the internet has many problems, but there aren't many days when I don't marvel at it's power to spread knowledge and goodness around the world.

---

[48] Unsplash - *https://unsplash.com/*

@emmaking   Emma King

Supporting teaching and learning in HE - interested in effective use of technology enhanced learning and teaching spaces (real and virtual). Coventry, UK

It's probably fair to say that I'm a late adopter. Whilst I am aware of the new technologies as they emerge I'm slow to adopt and have to see a real need for it before committing and buying. I often tell the story of being a teacher when smartboards were introduced and watching everyone just use them like a different type of whiteboard, and this encapsulates my perception of technology. It has to have a clear purpose. However, like David [Hopkins], if I had more money I'd probably have a lot more gadgets, but there's a chance I would either be leaving some of them at home or only using each one for a particular function.

Pen and notepad: I carry these everywhere I go and love to make handwritten notes, although they have to be in blue pen (not too sure why). Writing information down by hand helps me to remember and also lets me quickly find key points in my notes in a way I've not yet mastered with the typed word.

However, if I know that I will need to write the notes up afterwards then I swap and use my LiveScribe[49] pen and notepad, that via the iPad, allows me to quickly translate handwritten notes into text. You can also make an audio recording that helps when trying to remember exact detail, if people are happy to be recorded that is.

Tablet: My iPad Mini is always in my bag, and I love it. I use it for three key functions: searching for information, carrying 'papers' rather than taking hard copies, and taking photos of outcomes of discussions. If you picked my iPad up however you'd notice that it's full of different apps, normally downloaded to share new tools that colleagues might be interested in, whether I use them or not. (But interestingly if I really want to take photos I still carry a camera despite the fact the technology is probably way older than my phone).

In terms of my app use then I tend to use one tool for one purpose. I realise this isn't efficient and perhaps I need to develop my practice in this area. For example, I use Evernote to carry meeting papers and make notes as I mark so that I can move between home and work seamlessly, but I tend to use OneNote for capturing my thoughts as I study and learn. Similarly, if I need a tool for a new job then I end up searching for a new app, rather than investigating what the apps I already use might be able to do.

Phone: I carry my smartphone whenever I leave home. I use it for reading my email, home and personal, picking up messages, keeping my calendar and tracking health and fitness. However, having my work email on my phone means

---

[49] LiveScribe - *https://www.livescribe.com/*

I'm tempted to read it when I'm not at work as well, I've got much better at not replying, but I still read them. It's not that I'm worried if I am out of the loop, but more like some morbid fascination. I meant to take off my work email before my last week off, but somehow never quite did it. Perhaps next time... Interestingly the one time you might not get hold of me is when I'm at home as the phone will be abandoned somewhere in the house. This is quite freeing.

Glasses: I had forgotten these were technology to be honest, unless I'm in the pool they are permanently on my head.

Watch: I only wear a watch when I'm out, I need access to a clock particularly when I'm teaching. As soon as I get into the office though the watch goes onto my desk, and it's the same at home. We are surrounded by so many clocks I don't need one on my arm, and it gets in the way of typing. If I'm in the garden I'm lucky enough to be able to keep track of time through the village church bell.

Saying that, the one piece of technology I keep thinking about buying is a smartwatch. I switch between wanting one and thinking that I don't need that much information on my wrist. Do I really need to quantify my life? I'm not sure but I quite like the idea for running and swimming.

Kindle: I love reading and used to say I only read on paper. However, after being given a kindle I've found that it helps me to read more regularly. The ability to adjust the size of text to make it easier is a real advantage. Reference books still need to be in paper format however to allow me to flick to the relevant section and page quickly, there's something about a physical book that makes this so much easier.

iPod: I always have an iPod in my bag but actually rarely listen to it. If it is loud in the office, I'll put it on for a song but normally turn it off halfway through as I can't focus with the music playing either. It's great for listening to a comedy show when on a lunchtime walk though, and I happily chuckle away to myself much to the bemusement of anyone I might see.

Finally, I'd say that one 'ration' that I can't live without is an **internet connection**. This is my most important ration, to keep in touch with the world, find my way to places and of course shopping. It's amazing how frustrating a slow connection can be, and whilst generally not a problem at work if there's two of us trying to use it at the same time at home it can be painfully long winded trying to open a web page, and let's not talk about trying to stream a video. I can't wait for the day when we might get fibre.

So quite a basic list of technologies, nothing revolutionary. Despite there being just a core set here I'd still like to go on more of a digital diet: not read my work email when I'm at home, and not browsing the internet on my iPad when I'm watching the TV. The older I get the more I appreciate being technology free/light.

@nickotdV   **Nick Overton**

Teacher (KS2) V Dan @*leicestertkd* Taekwon-Do instructor. @*UKEd_EMids* ambassador. College of Teaching advocate. Thinker. The Yoda of education am I! Leicester, UK

As I am quite young many people thought that I would be quite dependent on technology. Well, so did I! But as I sit here and racked my brain I suddenly find the list isn't as long as I thought it would be. Furthermore, I like to think that I am quite a simple person, so I do have gadgets etc. but they are to improve my standard of living. When I leave the house, I have the following with me that are techy.

iPad: The iPad I use for school. It belongs to school but I use it at home too. I have a variety of apps on here that I use with the children. The main reason I use this is communication. I access my email from here, as I get anything from 10-15 a day, I like to be well informed. The apps can be put onto the Interactive whiteboard although I do not do this often as I find the connection process difficult with the software my school has. I use my iPad also to help me take notes during staff meeting and to help groups of Children. I sometimes use it instead of printing out worksheets. (I put the work onto the school drop box account and then they can access it and use the iPad instead of paper).

iPhone: My iPhone is the main techy item that I just could live without! I use it all the time and I currently have it sat next to me. I do not really keep up with modern technology so my phone is an old iPhone 4s. It is nearly 3 years old and is still going strong; as the saying go, why replace something that is not broken!

I use the following apps the most ...

Twitter: I use twitter in all areas of my life. I have a personal account that I use to discuss, talk about life, education etc. I run 2 professional accounts in which I promoted 2 significant areas of my life. The personal account is where I do the most tweeting. I would say that I am a prolific tweeter as I can see the benefits of communicating via this means. I have made many connections and these connections have led to some really interesting ventures. My 2 professional accounts are for the East Midland branch of the #UKEdChat group and for the Leicester Taekwon-Do academy; where I am the principal instructor.

I find twitter is a really good way of getting information that is painless and normally so quick. Twitter provides a vast community who thinks the same and often holds the same values. They are like a community group that you have never met but you are sure if you did, you would enjoy their company. As I have developed this role I am now meeting more of these people in real life and it often makes the meeting easier as we normally know something about each other before we meet (Like a blind date but we are not so blind anymore).

WhatsApp and Messenger: I come from a large family. I am 1 of 5 children and a few of my siblings have their own families. For this very reasoning, keeping in touch is very important. I know this will be the same for a lot of people but I like to know what's going on (I think this is something that is common amongst teachers, we do not like being left out of the loop). I also use it professionally to coordinate the running my Taekwon-Do club. I find emails/WhatsApp massagers are far more effective than putting all the information into a newsletter (although I still publish a monthly newsletter for my club). I also use it to keep in touch with friends who no longer live in the UK.

Weather: I am an avid walker. I really love getting into the countryside and exploring all the delights of nature. For this very reason, I like to know exactly what I will be faced with. I wouldn't say I am a fair-weather walker but I like to know if it is going to rain so that I am ready for it and prepared enough that I do not get ill. I also like to know if the weather is going to change as there is nothing worse than planning a picnic and then having to eat in the car because it is raining!

At home, I have an Apple Mac computer that I do most of my work on a Laptop that I use to support me as not all applications etc. are accessible from a Apple device. Apart from that my home is quite tech free. I have a standard TV with a Standard DVD player attached (No Blu-Ray here). We have no other TV's in the house; The Dining room is tech free and we believe that this is how it should be (eating should be a social time for talking and sharing; not watch TV). In the bedrooms, there is no tech a part from chargers for our respective phones. Both of us do not have Kindles and we both prefer to have books that have paper pages in them. I do not have an iPod and I play my music through the TV or the computer from a good old fashion 4GB USB stick.

In summary we live in quite a traditional house with an average amount of technology.

I started this my saying that it thought I was quite a techy person, turns out I am but with very few actual devices.

@julianstodd   **Julian Stodd**

Author   'Social   Leadership   Handbook'   [*http://goo.gl/CuKDri*]
Founder @*SeaSaltLearning*. Sometime artist. Occasional thinker. UK

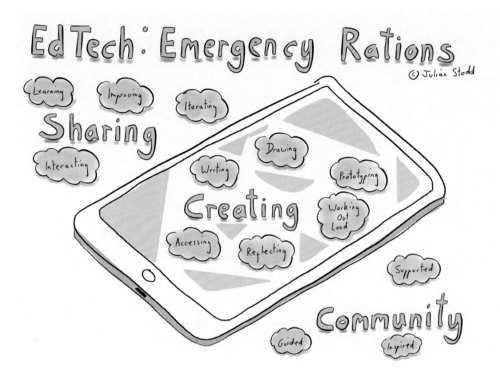

It's quite a challenge to identify my essential technology, the gadgets that I would not leave home without, the things which are indispensable. I find myself torn between the two halves of my persona: on the one side, the technophile, the gadget freak, the kleptomaniac of updates and new toys, and on the other side of the equation, the backpacking traveller who has a secret fetish for lightweight travel bags and an obsessive-compulsive tendency to travel with nothing but one lightweight spare pair of socks and a pencil.

I suspect if you are reading this book that you have little interest in my Eagle Creek rucksack collection, so I'm going with the first option, unleashing my obsessive technologist within, and listing those technologies I cannot leave home without, and possibly a few that I hope to be carrying sometime in the near future.

My iPad has to be top of the list: I'm currently sporting the iPad Pro, the oversized tablet that sits at the heart of my creative output. I illustrate using it every day, and the illustrative process has transformed my writing, making it (I hope) more accessible, and certainly shared far more widely.

I draw exclusively using the Paper app[50] on the iPad: it's indispensable to me, simple, open, and effortless. I'm not sure if I can justifiably go into this level of detail in a technology chapter, if I make the assumption that you are interested in choice of stylus, I use three.

My first choice is the Wacom Bamboo stylus[51] (in orange), which is a blunt soft tip, very forgiving, very durable. I must have six of these.

Secondly, I use the Pencil made by 53, the beautiful wooden stylus with Bluetooth functionality made by the same people that make the Paper app. When this is activated, it unlocks a different set of blending behaviours which I use almost exclusively when drawing 3D elements, especially the spheres which I use quite widely in my illustration. For the real nerds amongst you, I also used it for all the shading underneath the hand drawn lettering in the second edition of the Social Leadership Handbook[52], as it gives a much finer yet denser type of shadow, which I think looks better.

The third stylus is the newest, the Apple one, which is hard and white and, I have to say, my least favourite. It's the one I don't carry around very often. Personally, I find the hard tip difficult, my writing tends to be worse with it, and the tapping annoys me, but I'm still in an experimental phase, and I may find a use for it alongside the others.

The other apps I use almost constantly are Twitter and Slack, Twitter to communicate with my external community, and Slack which we use to run Sea Salt Learning with, as a virtualised organisation: it allows me to communicate with my team of 10 around the world and collaborate effectively on projects. Indeed, alongside the Sea Salt Learning team, I'm in around eight other Slack communities.

If I had written this chapter a year ago, I would have been writing it on the iPad, using a separate Bluetooth keyboard, but I have made one key change in the last year: I almost exclusively dictate my writing using the Dragon software[53] on a MacBook Air. On the plus side, this arrangement has almost banished the repetitive strain injury that, coupled with an old sailing injury, had seriously cramped my output. On the downside, I now travel almost everywhere with both iPad pro and MacBook Air, complete with both their chargers, and often travel adapters to go with them. So, I've lost something in terms of weight saving, but certainly gain something in terms of productivity.

Another piece of technology that is rarely out of my sight as my iPhone: you will

---

[50] Paper by 53 - *https://www.fiftythree.com/*

[51] Wacom Bamboo - *http://bamboo.wacom.com/*

[52] The Social Leadership Handbook (2nd ed.) - *http://seasaltlearning.com/books-2/*

[53] Dragon Dictate - *http://www.nuance.com/dragon/*

have realised by now that I'm firmly wedded to the Apple family, enjoying as I do the "it just works" functionality. At least, my needs, it just works.

The most utilised part of the iPhone is probably the camera: I am an obsessive photographer, indeed in a previous life I have run a number of exhibitions, one of my main current interests is graffiti. I probably gather around a thousand images a year as I travel around the world, indeed one of my favourite activities in new cities is to find the parts of town where graffiti abound.

Beyond this, my core ecosystem, we move to the technologies that are used less frequently. My Apple watch spends 90% of its time with a flat battery on my desk: it fails to integrate into my life, and now lies neglected. I use an Up Move fitness tracker[54], which I love (although which constantly gets me into trouble at airport security when I forget to take it off), and with that in place I find little use for the Watch.

As you may know, I was an obsessive early adopter of Google Glass[55], and will be an obsessive early adopter of the next generation when it lands, but for now, it's consigned to a draw. I happily spent months walking around London and other cities around the world wearing Glass with my prescription lenses in, and never experienced anything other than extreme curiosity. It certainly got me into a lot of conversations! You probably won't find me sporting the new Snapchat glasses any time soon, fashion icon as I am. I know my limitations.

It may surprise you to know that I almost never read e-books: I find I really cannot stand them. This may hark back to an earlier life when I ran a research library in a mediaeval building, and certainly speaks to my current housing arrangements which see an ongoing battle between the volume of books and my need to find a clear route to the front door. I am an obsessive purchaser of new books, believing in the osmotic principle of reading by association and proximity. Books I guess still count as technology, at least if I'm desperate enough.

My most recent technology is a Lego MindStorms robot[56], something which I've been working on with my niece and nephew as I try to stay a few days ahead of them as they learn to program. Truth be known, they are already overtaking me, and I have a sneaking suspicion that the robot knows this and simply tolerates my ineffectual prodding.

Finally, music. If I splash out on anything, it's a really superb record player, for evenings spent listening to vinyl at home, and really superb headphones to travel with. A lifetime of live music has left me with less than perfect hearing, and I have no problem spending on good headphones. Spending 35 weeks on the road last year was transformed with a decent pair of noise cancelling

---

[54] Up Move Fitness Tracker - *https://jawbone.com/fitness-tracker/upmove*

[55] Google Glass - *https://www.google.co.uk/intl/en/glass/start/*

[56] Lego MindStorms - *https://www.lego.com/en-gb/mindstorms*

headphones which transform the experience of travel.

Whatever technology you use, whatever you own emergency rations, I hope you find, as I have, that great technology democratizes and liberates creativity, let's you achieve far more than you could ever do without it.

@S_J_Lancaster   **Simon Lancaster**

European, Professor of Chemical Education, National Teaching Fellow, MOOC facilitator and cyclist. My tweets are my personal views not those of my institution. Norwich, UK

I have resisted the temptation to explore what emergency rations means to the geeky amateur cyclist. Instead, I seem destined to interpret the expression through the lens of a geeky iOS 'MAMIL' (Middle Aged Man In Lycra) with clinically diagnosed OCD (Obsessive Compulsive Disorder).

While I am confessing my deficiencies: after decades with 20:20 vision it pains me to need to use glasses. Fortunately, Apple did see me coming and have evolved from the 3.5" 3GS to the 5.5" iPhone 6S Plus at about the same rate as my eyesight has deteriorated. While smartphones may have expanded dramatically during this time-frame, clothes designers do not appear to have noticed. I can no longer fit my iPhone into the breast pocket of my shirt. Actually, on reflection, maybe clothes designers know what they are doing. If I put it in my trouser pocket it ruins my natural lines and I have to worry that it will bend. The 6S Plus is therefore often relegated to my bag, the most physically remote phone I've had since I succumbed to the siren ringtone of my first (T-Mobile) Nokia.

You will recall that I have OCD. Mine manifests itself as a fear of leaving things unlocked, switched on or misplaced. You cannot misplace a phone in a pocket but out of touch is out of (my) mind.

So my emergency ration is the solution to the disadvantages of a phablet. The Apple Watch. I am sympathetic to those early reviewers of the Apple Watch who criticised its dependence on the tethered iPhone. They bemoaned the lack of a killer application. For me, the little red icon at the top of the screen is the killer application. No longer do I have to scramble through my pockets, my bag or my desktop clutter for my mobile phone. If the icon is there, then my phone is nearby. My phone is safe.

It might be tethered through Bluetooth but the Apple Watch has liberated me from my iPhone. I no longer have to go to the terrible inconvenience of opening the case and resting my index finger on the home button if I want to check my alerts. A quick flick of the wrist and the BBC have brought me the latest ghastly tragedy to befall my football team. Although quite why Twitter think saying "Hi" to a new follower is a good idea escapes me.

How close am I to my Apple Watch? If it comes off during waking hours, it's either to even the tan or avoid flicks of paint. Sensible and reasonable, I am sure you will agree. So how about the ghostly haptics? Someone else tell me this is a 'thing'. If I take my watch off I will still experience the familiar tapping sensation that tells me something has happened. When I look down, that piece of me is missing like a first world imitation of a phantom limb.

What do university professors and road cyclists have in common? They are obsessed with metrics. The Apple Watch feeds our need for numbers: how fast our hearts are beating; how many calories we've burnt and how many miles traversed. Is it ironic that at exactly this point in the writing the haptics alert me that it is an hour since I stood up?

Would I starve without my Apple Watch? No. Would my productivity be dramatically reduced without it? No. Will I buy the next edition? If they add a gesture-activated wrist camera, definitely.

@EricStoller   **Eric Stoller**

Education consultant & speaker. Teaching social media & digital identity. Write for *@InsideHigherEd*. Live: UK. Work: Globally. London, UK

I don't always have to have the latest and greatest gadget. My focus has always been to acquire technology that lasts for a long time. My first MacBook Pro lasted for 5 years before I gave it away to a friend. My current machine is a year away from that record. My technology "rations" have been fairly consistent over the years. It's always best to keep things simple when you're an education consultant[57].

Time, Cuffs, and Distance
Work Watch: Having never tried on a watch with a metal mesh band before, I was quite skeptical of the Skagen Titanium[58]. However, it's become my primary watch for work. It's super low profile design works well with any shirt or jacket and the gunmetal titanium colour literally matches with anything in my wardrobe. And, it's unbelievably durable. I've replaced the battery in it on multiple occasions, but the glass and titanium casing looks almost new after 10 years of regular wear.

Running Watch: When I started long distance running in 2010, I would keep time with a simple digital watch and then use Google Maps to measure the distance of a run. It wasn't an ideal process. Fast forward to 2013 when I signed up for a marathon and I knew that I needed a better way to track my mileage. I was at a shoe store that catered to runners and I saw a guy wearing a gigantic watch on his wrist. It was the Garmin Forerunner 610[59] and I've been running with one ever since that day. It's literally been with me for thousands of miles.

Packs and Pockets
Backpack: I lived in Oregon for 7 years and during the 5th year I discovered Timbuk2 backpacks. Made from extremely durable nylon, they seemingly last forever. I have two of them at the moment. One is gigantic and holds almost as much as a small travel suitcase. The other is my "business" backpack. It's sleek and the laptop compartment is lined with red corduroy fabric.

Laptop: My 15 inch MacBook Pro is four years old and I use it almost every single day of the year (except when I'm on holiday). It's a workhorse of a computer that is quite good for keynote presentations, PhotoShop projects, video editing, etc. However, when Apple comes out with a new version of the "MBP," I will be downsizing to the 13-inch edition...the screen on my current computer is great, but it is a bit heavy to be lugging around airports and train stations.

---

[57] Eric Stoller - *http://ericstoller.com/work*

[58] Skagen Titanium Watches - *http://www.skagen.com/gb/en/men/watches/titanium.html*

[59] Garmin Forerunner 610 - *https://www.amazon.co.uk/dp/B0050HKOXQ*

Headphones: The Shure 535[60] sound isolating headphones are ridiculously expensive. However, they provide audio fidelity that is better than any other headphone that I've ever owned. They fit in your ears like the studio monitors that professional musicians wear and you will never be able to go back to cheap headphones after listening to music via the 535s. I'm always listening to something via Spotify, iTunes, Pandora (US-based), etc. They are also great for Google Hangouts or Skype conversations because they block out outside noise.

Wireless Mouse: The MX Anywhere 2 wireless mouse from Logitech is absolutely the finest mouse I've ever used. The smooth scroll and "works on any surface" technology makes for a consistently enjoyable experience. And, it is rechargeable...no batteries required. While the touchpad is an okay option for surfing the web and basic tasks, I've always preferred the speed and precise control of a mouse.

Tablet: I've gotten a lot of use from my iPad. Purchased way back in 2012, it's got a few dents in it, but the retina display is still working well. If I'm going to be live-tweeting at a conference, I always use my iPad as it is so much quieter than my laptop (touchpad versus clickity-clack of keys).

Presentation Remote: If you frequently give presentations with a slide deck, a presentation remote is a must. When I started my consulting business in 2010, I bought a SMC-Link Remotepoint Navigator remote. It's probably the most important piece of technology in my backpack.

Kindle: My wife was given a Kindle Paperwhite[61] as a gift by a friend. On a flight from the UK to the US, I read a book on it and knew that I had to have one. With only a couple of minutes to spare at the Dallas/Fort Worth Airport, I found a technology vending machine that was selling the Paperwhite. It's the best piece of tech for long-form reading. There is not any glare and the size it perfect. Plus, the battery life is magical. It rarely requires a new charge.

Adaptors: There are all sorts of cables and adaptors in my backpack, but the most important ones are the display adaptors for my laptop. I carry a VGA and an HDMI adaptor in my bag. I give a lot of presentations and it's vital that I'm able to connect my MacBook Pro to the projector at an event. When I purchased a MacBook Pro for the first time in 2007, I didn't realize that I would need an adaptor to connect to LCD projectors. I flew halfway across the United States for a consulting engagement and didn't have a way to connect to a projector. Fortunately, the hotel that I was staying with had one on site. Since that day, I've always had this vital piece of kit in my backpack.

---

[60] Shure 535 Sound Isolating Earphones -
https://www.shure.co.uk/products/earphones/se535

[61] Amazon Paperwite - *https://www.amazon.com/dp/B00AWH595M*

Phone: My first smartphone was the Blackberry Storm. It was a wonderful paperweight. Switching over to an Android-based device after a "stormy" year, I upgraded to the Motorola DroidX. It was a wonderful phone. And yet, my computer was a Mac and I wanted to go Apple with everything. That's when I purchased an iPhone 5 with 64 gigabytes of storage space. It turns out that this particular iPhone that I purchased from an Apple store in Boston, Massachusetts in 2012 is compatible with US and UK mobile networks in 2016. All I have to do is swap my sim cards from my US provider to my UK provider and I can get fast, reliable, and inexpensive 4G mobile access.

Apps: There aren't a lot of apps that are "must haves" ... Twitter, Facebook, Instagram, LinkedIn, Reddit, YouTube, Snapchat, Medium, Periscope ... they are awesome. However, if I had to pick just 5 apps that are absolutely necessary, I would go with: Google Maps, TripIt Pro[62], Uber (in the US), Hailo[63] (in the UK), and Apple's Music app.

---

[62] TripIt Pro Travel App - *https://www.tripit.com/pro*

[63] Hailo - *https://www.hailoapp.com/*

@BryanMMathers   **Bryan Mathers**

Helping others to think visually. Founder of *@wearewapisasa*, *@visualthinkery* and co-founder of *@weareopencoop*. Mostly CC-BY-ND. London, UK

EMERGENCY RATIONS

HAVE BAG CAN WORK

@bryanMMathers

CABLES
(you know the sort –
Apple adapters,
usb chargers,
hdmi cables, etc)

iPAD
(for drawing
stuff like this)

iPAD MINI
(for all things work and
anything that
buzzes –
trello
twitter
slack
drive...)

WIRELESS MOUSE
(full control
on the hoof)

MACBOOK PRO
(for putting stuff together)

Rookie

VISUAL
THINKERY

A FEW GOOD PENS
(ones that allow thoughts
to flow)

TWO
SKETCHBOOKS
(current and
previous)

EARPHONES
(the world is
too noisy)

iPHONE
(for all things personal –
audible
citymapper
receiptbank
carbo
podcasts
music...)

BAG STUFF
paracetamol
lip salve
post-its
stylus
keys
cards

WATERPROOF BAG
(with loads of pockets)

@milenabobeva   **Milena Bobeva**

MBA Director, Principal Lecturer, CMgr FCMI, SFHEA. Bournemouth, UK

Nosce te ipsum. ("Know thyself")

An audit of the emergency (tech) rations I keep has turned into an interesting journey of self-discovery. I have accepted that such introspection is only natural, given that for the larger part of my life I have been an advocate of systems thinking and systems practice[64]. Thus, even the most trivial musings about technology, software application or other artefacts are done with consideration of their context (or ecosystem), including stakeholders and associated behaviour and transformations.

Me, myself and I

I am a self-professed optimiser, always looking for a better, leaner, more agile, integrated and user-friendly solution. I am an early adopter of innovations[65], eager to test technologies that could bring these benefits. This makes me a gadgeteer, always looking for the latest tools that will allow me to do more with less, i.e. things that add value and could positively influence my work-life balance. My passion for gadgets is kindled by my husband – he appreciates the challenge coming from my "I wish I could", and seeks solutions that would meet the expectations of a 'moderately' demanding techno-savvy user like me. I call this 'romantic'. We have shared the love for useful things and clever solutions bursting with functionality. It often happens that some of their features remain unexplored due to lack of time .... to read the manual in full. So, any tech ration in my view will have to be multi-functional and intuitive to use. All items in my survival kit are tested on both criteria.

The 24/7 survival kit

I would like to have a minimalist lifestyle, yet I would also like to be prepared for any situation, regardless whether I am OTG (On-The-Go) or at home. Therefore, my survival kit must allow for a mobile lifestyle. I am constantly searching for integrated light weight solutions, whether they are wearable technology or anything else that could fit in my over-the-shoulder handbag. And here is the list of these items that I carry with me every day:

Smartphone: The arrival of the smart phone has removed from my survival kit devices such as the mini Maglite torch, the MP4 player, voice recorder and the camera. The front camera would have probably also removed the vanity mirror, if it were not built into the lid of my makeup bag. I consider myself a smart shopper, who is more sensitive to functionality and price, than to brand names.

---

[64] Peter Checkland "Systems Thinking, Systems Practice"
https://www.amazon.co.uk/dp/0471986062

[65] Everet M Rogers "Diffusion of Innovations, 5th Edition"
https://www.amazon.co.uk/dp/0743222091

Yet, last Christmas, after more than 10 years with an Android phone, I have switched to an iPhone. Admittedly, this was not my decision, but a present – I guess that my husband, being tired of me moaning how my 1 year old HTC was running very quickly out of battery and has become very slow, asked 'Santa' to bring me an iPhone 6 S Plus 16GB that could synch seamlessly with the iPad I use for work (mostly) and the Apple devices our kids use.

I love my new phone and I hate it: love how it is integrated with the other devices and I hate having constantly to deal with messages about low storage space. I am bemused how my daughter could keep 12000 photos on her 64 GB phone and I can't. At least now I know that I should be monitoring eBay for a bargain on a 64GB or 128GB version. Or maybe I should wait until next Christmas. I know that now 'Santa' knows how important having sufficient memory on the phone, is for my wellbeing. ;-)

iPad Air: I got fascinated by the iPad back in 2011 when I took part in a project for evaluating different tablets we could use for sharing materials with students. Following the project, the Faculty bought a few devices to enable colleagues to optimise our work patterns. Now, on my second iPad, I blame (or thank?) this gadget for all things Apple in my life. The tablet is my library, entertainment system, relaxation centre, communication channel with the rest of the world. And it has sufficient memory (for now). The kids are sometimes embarrassed with me, as I use it to take photos when my phone runs out of space. I wish I had the Air 2 because of the biometrics security system, but the new features are not sufficient justification for the investment I must make. Even though it is the almost as capable as my Toshiba Portege i7 lightweight laptop.

Smartwatch: I never thought that I will replace my automatic waterproof big-brand-name Swiss watch to a plastic electronic one, until my husband decided that I need to be reminded how little I sleep and got me a Sony SWR30 smart watch. And I loved it immediately – lightweight, multi-functional, even with different colours straps (in case one has time to change these). I would see who is calling me, read messages, take phone calls, know how many steps I walked that day. And it was all good until I had to change from an Android phone to an IOS one. Within the year I had the watch, Sony has already released a new version, and the old one was not compatible with the IOS. Any IOS app that worked with the SWR30 cut off some of the functionality of the watch.

The Apple Watch that was just released at the time, seemed like a good replacement, but it seemed very expensive, it was not waterproof and, most of all, I did not want other to see me as one of these fashion followers. However, being a bargain-hunter I could not miss a good deal when it comes my way and when I saw a real bargain from an online retailer from a 3-days lighting deal, I surrendered and bought my first Apple Watch. With the second series that is waterproof recently released, I am now considering an upgrade – at least I won't have to worry taking it off before I go in the shower or for a swim

Pandora+ bracelet: This another of the items that have been with me for more than 5 years now. It started as a family present with a few Pandora charms that remind me of what is important in life and how much my family means to me. It keeps me positive in difficult times and these days could double up as a weightlifting bracelet or a type of bell shaker percussion instrument. As I could not resist adding a couple of non-Pandora rich in symbolism charms it is now a Pandora+ bracelet.

Keyring bundle: This is the bundle attached to my small soft leather purse that doubles as a key ring/key holder. For the past 25 years, it content has been almost unchanged. It includes:

- The house keys and the key to my cupboard at work
- Classic SD Swiss-army (Victorinox) knife
- 3-way USB charger cable
- Mini tablet stylus that doubles as a pen
- Two USB flash drives: a small 8GB that works on every machine and a 32GB solid state key that for some (probably very basic) reason is not recognised by some machines
- £1 coin for the supermarket trolley
- A few mini store/membership cards

Tech (mini) bag: This includes the corded ear phones, the Bluetooth ear-phones, a USB multi-card reader, an SD card reader micro 3-in-1 Lightning USB SDHC Micro SD Card Adapter, cleaning cloths, various adapters for cards and plugs.

My apps bundle: This will never be a full list, but here are the current favourites:

- **Storage and notes:** iCloud, DropBox, Google Drive
- **Notetaking:** Notes, Evernote, Google Keep
- **Communication:** Facetime, Skype, WhatsApp, WeChat, Viber, Media5-fone (internet-phone).
- **Social networks:** Facebook, LinkedIn, HootSuite, ScoopIt, Pinterest, Instagram, Twitter, SnapChat.
- **Edutainment:** IMDB, Kindle, iBooks, SoundHound, Spotify, Podcasts
- **Games:** Elevate, DuoLingo, Memrise.
- **Information services and shopping:** Weather, Maps, Google Translate, Live Collage, Amazon Prime (instant gratification), GroupOn

The 'Away from the Base' kit

This is the 'extension' of the 24/7 kit that I take on trips that last from one day up to 3 weeks (I have not tested this for longer):

- A choice of two power banks: a lighter one with 2 USB ports and an ultra-high capacity 20,000mAh one, with 4 ports
- Universal travel adapter with 4 USB ports and a couple more single socket travel adapters with an extension cube for 3 plugs
- Xiomi Yi camera[66] (GoPro equivalent) with all gadgets for any type of

activity
- A few SD, mini-SD and micro high capacity cards – it proved to be very useful when, due to the latest 'enhancement' from the central services, my laptop is having problems accessing my storage drive at work
- A spare unlocked phone with appropriate SIM card adapters that will allow me to turn the phone into an Internet hub by buying a local data-only card

The 'Away from Base' kit usually needs a small rucksack/trolley suitcase and spreads across several trays when offloaded in full at the airport security check up. If not offloaded, I usually have to go twice through the system or have it checked separately.

My biggest challenge is linked to consumerism and ethical values. I don't like the term 'hoarder' but cannot throw away things that are in good working order, even if I do not need then anymore. I try to recycle, sell or donate, but am yet to find how to do with technologies for the greatest return on investment or value for consumer. Because of this I still have a collection of old phones and laptops, and their accessories.

On a positive side, old phones come handy when I go abroad and I need a phone for a SIM for local calls or for the data-only card that will tether Internet connection to all other devices.

I guess the topic that I will be reading next will be on how to recycle your 'out-of-date' tech rations ☺

---

66 Xiaomi yi Camera Xiaoyi Action Sport Camera:
https://www.amazon.co.uk/dp/B00UFFZU06

@alexgspiers   **Alex Spiers**

Learning Technology Developer at the University of Liverpool. Co-ordinate #ALTNWESIG & member of #MELSIG Interested in mobile tech, social media & feedback. Liverpool, UK

I'm not a very gadgety person. It's almost a shameful admission for someone in my line of work, that I don't have the latest iPad, smartphone, games console, clever watch or VR thingamabob. If I'm honest, I tend to get more excited about new software rather than hardware. Apps, new platforms, new ways of working, connecting, collaborating and playing is where I become enthused. It's complicated when you think about how you connect and consume all these things. And I'm still a huge fan of things – physical things. At this point in my life, perhaps due to habit but not wholly so, I still buy my music on Vinyl & CD. Movies tend to be bought in DVD format and I still buy good old paper books to add to the hoards we have in the loft and elsewhere around my house. I like to switch the TV on and serendipitously watch whatever is on at the time, but I do also love my box sets and short YouTube shows. My magazine subscription comes with a digital iPad app which is great for searching articles, but I still get most enjoyment from reading the paper version once it's been popped through my letterbox each month – a forgotten present. That said, 2016 has been the year that I have spent the most money of digital 'stuff' – subscriptions, cloud storage, media content etc. As I said, it's complicated. Long live Physical Media! Long live Digital Media!

Wearables
Glasses: The type of technology I normally forget about as I, as well as friends and family, see glasses as actually part of my face. They are almost part of the physical make up of my face and certainly a tangible part of my identity. I feel quite naked without them. Most folk I know don't like to see me without them and I'm too squeamish for contacts. I don't upgrade too often and the look changes very minimally. Black, square and boxy. None of those fashionably big ones for me.

Watch: I have periods when I wear a watch and times when I don't. My wrists are naked at the moment due to losing my MUJU watch. Which is a shame, as it was a lovely minimal design. A dumb watch with no numbers or apps. I say wear because it's really only a bit of jewelry. Like many of you, I no longer need a watch to tell the exact time. I'm surrounded by devices and tools that inform me of hours, mins, & secs. – The clock in my car, my mobile devices, church bells ringing near my office and the gentle, hourly Zen tone emanating from my colleague's phone.

Headphones: I'm not wandering around town with oversized Beats headphones. My cheap and cheerful array of in-ear headphones suit me just fine. I'm not an audiophile and in any case I lose so many pairs of these things it wouldn't be practical. This technology is essential for many areas of my life. I never travel on public transport without having my headphones and a bunch of music to listen to. At work, music helps me concentrate and be productive. Even the act of putting headphones gets me to focus on the task at hand.

In my pocket
I don't carry a wallet so it tends to be just coins, notes and cards. Oh yes, and my mobile of course. Inside left or jeans back right. I've never lost a phone as I'm a little OCD about where it is at all times.

Phone: In my line of work I find it's important to be able to speak two mobile languages: Android and Apple. My phone is always Android and my tablets are always Apple. I've stuck with Samsung for the past three phones (S2, S3 & A5). Choosing a phone tends to pivot around the camera spec and the cost. Contracts over £25 a month for a phone don't interest me and I would never purchase one outright. I like to change every two years and I'm patient enough that I don't need the latest features on the first day of release anyway. Life it too short to be queuing up outside a phone shop waiting for the new release.

What do I use my phone for? Note taking, photos, social media, email, listening to music, the odd text and occasional phone call. Just the usual stuff I guess. I don't have my whole music collection on my phone because it doesn't have that much space. In any case, I much prefer to download and listen to things in small chunks. With Spotify I get paralysed by the tyranny of choice, so I make sure I add a little – listen to it, and repeat.

In my bag
I do carry a bag around a lot. Sometimes it doesn't have much in it. Other times it's packed. It's a scruffy looking thing but does the job. I also have a "man bag" which I really only use at conferences. Looks nice and keeps laptops, phones and changer safely locked away.

Chargers: Phone and iPad chargers go everywhere with me. I'm always on the scrounge for more power wherever I am. Most people tend to be very accommodating about this these days.

Tablet: I have three iPads, which all still work to a greater or lesser degree. My iPad one is a heavy relic from an early period of mobile tech. Still connects to the internet but there are few apps that work on it these days. The kids don't even use it but I'm still fond it. I was fortunate to win an iPad mini at the Durham Blackboard conference a few years back. This was my main tablet until I recently replaced it with iPad Air 2. I toyed with the notion of getting the larger one but found it too big, and do I really need an £80 Apple Pen? This one will last me a few years and they I'll see what else is available. I do lots of things on my iPad – see apps below.

Laptop: I have an HP EliteBook running Windows 7 which is connected to a second screen on my standing desk in my office. I access all the programs you would expect on this: Office suite, Evernote, Chrome, Screencastomatic[67],

Skitch, Dropbox, and occasionally Slack, Skype. I'm writing this longer document on it as I'm still only doing short-ish bits of work on the iPad.

My nine essential apps

Does anyone really need 9 essential apps? Perhaps it is too much but I really do use these apps every single day to make my home and work life more effective and simpler. On the whole:

Twitter: is the keystone of my working practice. Notifications are always one (except when I Digitally Detox each year), it's my go to area for help, publishing, sharing, connecting, support, inspiration, news, ideas, and is the start and end of the day.

Evernote (premium account): The main reason for taking up Evernote was that I ended up with a pile of half started notebooks and never seemed to have the right one, for the right meeting. Having all my notes, but also my to do lists, reminders, articles, back up emails, presentations, research ideas all in one, searchable place is just essential to how I exist at this time. Add to that, web clipper and text encryption and the fact is is all your data – not being harvested for advertisers. You can delete your whole account and no trace will be left. Unusual these days...

Facebook: 21st Century problems. I love and loathe this app. I install it on my phone and remove regularly and I hate having to use their messenger app. The extreme side of me wants to download all my photos I've shared over the years and wrap the whole thing up. Leave it empty and ghostlike. However, it's those friendships that make it so difficult to get rid of. I don't use Facebook for work, only for family, friends and long-lost folk I used to know in another country. Some of these people I haven't seen for 10 years or so, don't know their address let alone phone number but it's great share (albeit in a small way) our joys in this space. Even though Facebook pushes me advertisements, it mistreats my privacy and sells my data, I find the pull of the people irresistible and so I keep coming back to your simple blue interface. Damn you Zuckerberg! Damn my weak will!

WhatsApp: Only recently become useful. I have a group of friends that refuse to answer emails, FB messages etc. but for some reason they use this. My use of it has grown the more mainstream it has become.

Dropbox (premium account): Most things I have digitally reside in Dropbox. For me, it's simple and easy to use, cross platform and reliable. I take lots of photographs and I love the automatic upload feature which backs up my images without me having to do anything. I also have a further backup in Flickr using the same feature. Up until recently, I was happy to just use the free allocation plus the additional storage space I received when I introduced new users. I was an early adopter so was able to secure 26GB for free. That's become too small for

---

[67] Screencast-O-Matic - *http://screencast-o-matic.com/home*

my current needs.

Skitch Desktop: Part of the Evernote eco system. At first I thought it would be a useful tool for annotating PDFs in Evernote. However, I've not really taken to it as there are better apps for that now (Adobe, iAnnotate). Where it really has come into its own is creating help guides and PowerPoint presentations. The screengrab functionality is simple and easy, saves as PNG and can have arrows and text added to it. At least once a day I will chop something up using this tool.

Google Fit & Runtastic Pro: Google Fit is a relative newcomer to the lucrative health app marketplace. I like that is I free, works as a pedometer where you can set targets, view your personal bests and it can suck in data from other fitness apps such as Runtastic. I've been using this for 4 years and was reluctant to move to something else. This integration means I don't have to.

Google Play, iTunes, MixCloud, Spotify & YouTube: I listen to A LOT of music. In lots of different situations so I need access to lots of different ways to listen. I still download a little so I can listen on the go. I'm not keen on streaming music when out and about. Too tight with my data I guess.

@steve_collis   **Steve Collis**

Education guy, 2002-2016. It's been a blast! For now, it's goodbye. Sydney, Australia

For me these technologies are more than tools: they are natural extensions of myself: my physical movement, my cognition, my very intentionality.

Wearables
Carbon-fibre ankle braces: First thing first: can I walk? I have Charcot-Marie-Tooth disease (CMT), which slows down my peripheral nervous system and turns walking into a tight-rope exercise. With weak ankles and severe foot drop, I'm grateful to the German company Ottobock, who provide lightweight ankle-braces that fit in my shoes and hug my lower legs with Velcro. Sitting at a right-angle, they support my ankles and stabilise my walking.

Shoes: The challenges of my CMT have lead me to an extreme minimalism: an acute appraisal of what is, and isn't worth bothering with. Knowing this, how many items of footwear do you think I might own? Include in your estimate slippers, sandals, dress shoes, sneakers, and so forth. I can tell you that I own very few indeed.

Make a guess at how few, then read on.

The answer is that I own one pair of shoes and no other footwear at all. The shoes are black comfy sneakers that almost (but not really) pass for dress shoes. They get along very well with my ankle braces and that's all I care about. So, come rain, shine, jungle treks or a beach stroll, movie night or high tea with the queen, my footwear is steady, constant, and often inappropriate to the context.

BOSE QC10 Sound Reduction Headphones: In a world of overwhelming information overload, I dislike noise of both the literal and figurative kinds. To deal with literal noise, I have headphones that reverse and rebroadcast incoming sound waves to cancel them out before they get to me.

Mack's Earplugs: For deeper serenity, I double-up the headphones with bulk-buy foam earplugs. I buy them in tubs of 100. Combined with the headphones, they create deep silence for me, so I can order my thoughts before someone else does it for me.

In my pocket
Minimalist Wallet: Reading "The Life Changing Joy of Tidying Up" by Marie Kondo did nothing to help my minimalism (as Joyce Seitzinger has mentioned already in this collection of #EdTechRations). My wallet is simply my phone case with a driver's license and two EFTPOS cards squeezed in.

Evernote and the "Getting Things Done" Method: Ten years ago, I read a workflow book called "Getting Things Done" by David Allen, and my life changed overnight and forever. His core suggestion is to capture and tag all the moving parts of life into one unified reflective system.

My everything-system is Evernote. I often capture items using the Evernote app on my phone. An item could be a crazy idea in the middle of the night, a bill to pay, a piece of research pertinent to a project, a bucket-list ambition, or contact information for a client or colleague.

I'm constantly capturing throughout the day. In mid-conversation, I'll capture an item. In the middle of the night, I'll capture an item. While driving the car I'll use Siri to dictate an item. My email inbox floods me with over 100 potential items each day. All these items, once captured, land in a holding folder in my Evernote account. When I'm at a laptop I sort each item out. Is it reference material? Is it an action item? Is it a new project to undertake? Is it a "someday/maybe" item that, for the moment, just needs incubating.

It takes time to process this extensive list of amorphous opportunities, obligations and rabbit holes of inquiry. This time amounts to something like a therapy session. I learned from Allen that the agreements we make with ourselves are not forgotten by our unconsciousness, and hover like a cloud. As I process new items and review existing ones, I'm cleaning out my cerebral RAM until it's defragmented and crystal clean. Once I'm emerged from this daily habit, I have clarity. I know what I'm doing, and what I'm not doing.

It doesn't matter how extensive my to-do list is, once it's been quantified and clarified it loses its bite. I'm the master of my workflow. There is no gap between what I think I ought to be doing and what I am actually doing. Thanks, David Allen, and thanks Evernote for that revolution!

In my bag
Three Moleskine Notebooks + One Ballpoint Pen: The three notebooks are quite small (13 x 21cm) and thin. Each has a different title and purpose. From the "Shitty First Drafts" (for uncensored stream-of-consciousness personal journaling) to the "Visioning and Planning" notebook (for general notes, ideas and plans) . and the "Boot Up" (a carefully crafted notebook which I read and reflect on each morning before leaving home. It contains reminders to me about who I am and what really matters to me. I add to it only very slowly) my notebooks are very important to me.

I use sketchnoting techniques to bring clarity to my thoughts, and often add the sketchnotes to my universal system using Evernote.

A Surface Pro Computer: My laptop is barely larger than an iPad, can act like a tablet with a detachable keyboard, and fits neatly into my discreet man-bag. It plugs happily into a big computer screen when I'm at home or work, but is just small enough that I am permitted to use it during takeoff and landing when flying.

@jennifermjones   **Jennifer M Jones**

Digital Media Educator & ethnographer. *#open* Web& social media, digital storytelling, events & citizen journalism. PhD *#Van2010*. Greyhounds. *#jisc50social*. Glasgow, UK

Over the last 10 years, I have been interested in 'digital storytelling' and 'citizen journalism' - what gives certain people the authority to tell stories on behalf of others - and how the person in the street - can learn to produce and share their stories using mobile and digital media.

I've been balancing my work practice as a portfolio career - working between higher education, the public and the third sector - as a researcher, digital media practitioner and educator. I have taught the focus of my research and practice of citizen journalism to many different people outside and within the university, with community groups, marginalised communities and activist settings.

I have to admit; I'm not driven by the need to own or be loaded down by the latest gadgets. Personally, the technology that I've used for work, play and to support others hasn't changed for nearly 10 years. I carry an iPhone and a MacBook Pro. Albeit, an iPhone and MacBook Pro that I upgrade every couple of years. How original for a 'digital media practitioner.' I don't leave the house without them. I've only recently picked up an iPad Pro again - having passed on my original iPad to my 90-year-old grandpa at the start of 2014. These days the processor speeds and amazing quality of video capture (4k!) has meant that I'm using both the iPhone and iPad as part of my day to day work, balancing the data load between them both.

I always prefer to work remotely - I find it out to have to travel somewhere to plug in and do my job. This MacBook Pro and iPhone is my entire work set up. It's my office. It means I can work anywhere - and I prefer to work anywhere than be tied down to one desk and one desktop. I'm writing this chapter in the coffee shop under my flat - already today I've have moved from the kitchen, to the living room and finally down the stairs to switch up my workspace whilst keeping myself in writing mode. Too long in one place and I feel my attention waning.

It's the same for when I visit sites of work. There is no guarantee that I am going to be able to access the facilities as a visiting trainer. I need to be sure that I have equipment that allows me to undertake the training I have planned and the people I am going to be working with it have access to it. So I strip back rather than bulk up the hardware I carry with me. If I'm training groups in a particular skillset - such as 'citizen reporting'[68], I want them to feel that they can participate immediately without buying fancy kit or having a limitless budget. Similarly, many publicly-owned venues may have restricted access to websites

---

[68] Citizen Reporting: *http://civicactivism.buildingchangetrust.org/tools-directory/Citizen-Reporting*

and applications - there have been more one time where I've taught young people Twitter methods using post-it notes and biros. Those attending are often surprised that they won't be sitting at rows of PCs, learning digital tools through a set of steps and instructions. The focus, for me, needs to be on storytelling - and the learning comes with it.

Digital Storytelling and Citizen Journalism in practice

I was the project coordinator for two major event themed projects about citizen journalism; #citizenrelay[69] (covering the torch relay for London 2012 Olympic Games) and Digital Commonwealth[70] (a Scottish Government legacy from for Glasgow 2014 Commonwealth Games).

Both projects aimed to recruit and support volunteers to develop skills to allow them to become citizen journalists and to report on the local events happening in Scotland around both major sporting event.

When we began in January 2012, in order to deliver a project of this scale, whilst keeping it accessible, we thought we might have to supply the kit for all of our volunteers.

For #citizenrelay, we ended up working with 40 people from all over Scotland. What became quite clear was, that although funding allowed us to prepare kit bags, full of small pocket video cameras (the Kodak Playtouch[71], much like the discontinued Flip Cam[72] - but with a handy external mic socket) and accessories, such as a range of microphones (RODE, clip-on and boom) and tripods (Joby Gorillapods[73] were a particular favourite).

Despite our provision, many of our volunteers had their own equipment and preferred to use that instead.

The equipment that they all had was a smartphone. And that smartphone allowed them to create media on the go, perform basic edits and share it with the rest of the team on the go. Although the kit bags were there, the speed that they needed to create and share in order to stay on top of what was happening meant that there was no time to stop, download and edit. The kit, inevitably, ended up locked away in an office at the university, requiring somebody to sign it in and out of the cupboard - whilst the media produced by those taken part, that made it to the project website and archive, was made on what the participants had in their pockets.

---

[69] #citizenrelay. http://www.citizenrelay.net/

[70] Digital Commonwealth. http://www.digitalcommonwealth.co.uk/

[71] Kodak Playtouch. http://www.techradar.com/reviews/cameras-and-camcorders/camcorders/kodak-playtouch-929921/review

[72] Flip Cam. https://en.wikipedia.org/wiki/Flip_Video

[73] Joby Gorillapod. http://joby.com/gorillapod

It doesn't take much to turn your smartphone into the 'Swiss Army knife' of media making. A visit to your local pound shop will acquaint workshop participants with a 'selfie stick' - what was once a Monopod[74] - and for less than the price of your lunch, you have both a device to hold your phone steady - and a attachment that converts your phone to be screwed into any tripod on the market.

Similarly, the hands-free headphones that come with your phone can be used as a makeshift microphone (or have a look for smartphone microphones such as the iRig[75])- with the ability to listen and record sound at the same time.

Download a professional mobile video application like Filmic Pro[76] (between £2.99-£10) and you have control over your audio levels, white balance, focus and quality of footage.

However, what I like to emphasis is that all of this can be done with the phone already in your pocket - and it is less about the additional technology that you plug into it. The extra technology can improve the quality of your footage, allow you to improve your skills and take the next steps - but the exciting part is being able to do with the phone you have already.

When it comes to the emergency rations required for citizen reporting, I've operated under some guiding principles that I've learnt through working with people from all ages and backgrounds; *you should be able to use what is in your pocket already and focus on developing your practice rather than worrying about being on top of the technology.*

---

[74] Monopod. *https://en.wikipedia.org/wiki/Monopod*

[75] iRig. *http://www.ikmultimedia.com/products/irigmic/*

[76] Filmic Pro. *http://www.filmicpro.com/*

@nrparmar   Nitin Parmar

Digital Education Consultant *@LearningFive* | Football Development Systems Consultant & ECAS Tutor *@PremierLeague* | Senior Fellow *@HEAcademy* | ex-*@uniofbath* | *@BathRugby* Season Ticket Holder. Bath & London, UK.

A few days ago, curiosity got the better of me, where I parted with £12 and bought a Nokia 3210 phone from eBay. This pre-millennium mobile phone was my first: laced with a monochrome screen, the irreplaceable addictive game that was *Snake* and a battery that would last for days. SMS was coming to the fore – complete with a 10p charge for each 160-character text message and a free delivery report to confirm its safe receipt by the recipient.

One of my earliest memories of using this phone was to let my parents know that I had reached a gig at Wembley Arena safely. There was rarely a huge need to worry about running out of battery life on the phone or carry a multitude of cables or chargers from one place to the next. Or indeed, consider the availability of reliable 4G data connection or robust Wi-Fi to "check in" your location or post photos on social media platforms.

Fast forward eighteen years to 2017, where my work as a consultant ensures that whilst travelling nationwide regularly, having an appropriate collection of *#EdTechRations* within reach is essential. To me, staying connected my family and work is imperative when I am on the move and away from home. These encompass the following:

Apple iPhone 7 128gb: Quite clearly, one of the best devices that I have ever owned. It is the ultimate communication device that allows me to call (audio, FaceTime), send and receive email (Gmail, Outlook) and text messages (iMessage, SMS, Whatsapp), take and edit photos, interact with social media and business networks (Facebook, Instagram, Twitter, LinkedIn), listen to music (Spotify, iTunes) or the radio (BBC iPlayer Radio, Smooth, Magic), take notes (Apple Notes, Evernote), control my smart home (Sonos, Mobile Alerts, Kasa, Alexa) and manage files (Dropbox, Backblaze). All on the move. The knowledge that the content is being backed up regularly on Apple's iCloud is invaluable. As is two-factor authentication! This is all supported by EE's excellent 4GEE Extra plan, which includes a good allowance of monthly data (15gb) roaming throughout the EU without incurring extra changes. For those longer days, I switch phone cases to **Apple's Smart Battery Cover Case** for the extra power that it brings.

Apple iPad Pro 9.7" 256gb: Being part of, and buying into, Apple's ecosystem is that a user can move from one device to another almost seamlessly. When the iPhone screen feels too little, the ability to send iMessages and SMS on this tablet device is very useful. Or taking notes (as text and sketches) during a day of meetings or conference talks using the **Apple Pencil**. A day is rarely complete without dipping into the news (BBC News, The Times, The Evening Standard) or watching a missed episode (BBC iPlayer). The ability to download content for offline reading and viewing is essential the traveler, so I often consider why the user experience around this can be so poor. Where the data connection is more reliable, apps for watching live sport (Sky Go, BT Sport) when away from home offer exceptional value.

Apple MacBook Air 13" / 256gb SSD / 8gb Memory (mid-2013): Having been brought up on a healthy diet of Microsoft Windows-based PCs, the move to a Mac some time ago – first with a Mac Mini – was quite a shock to the system. However, through some persistence, compromise and adaptation, the Air is now an invaluable part of my armory, where I can now comfortably use it for business productivity as well as personal interests. I still use Microsoft Office for Mac though as the corporate environments that I work in are still very much Windows and Office based. Adobe Creative Cloud apps play an important role in my work as does software such as Camtasia, Handbrake, Photo Mechanic and VLC. The excellent battery life of the Air, which can get me through much of the day, lets me know that I rarely need to worry about finding a power socket at a client site or on the train. That said, I have three 45W MagSafe 2 Power Adapters which are often dotted in various locations around the country depending on where I am.

EE Osprey Mobile Broadband: Having briefly experimented with tethering data from my iPhone to my iPad or Air, I soon established that this just was not practical for a variety of reasons, such as the impact on battery life. The idea of being able to setup a mobile hotspot has become essential, especially when at client offices or spending nights in hotels where their own Wi-Fi is expensive or unreliable. Sky's inclusion of free access to The Cloud Wi-Fi hotspots within their Sky Fibre Max broadband package is useful too – particularly when having lunch in Wagamama.

Beats by Dr. Dre Headphones: I have two sets of headphones which I use depending on their scenario of use. The Tour 2.0 in-ear headphones (with the additional **Apple 3.5mm to Lightning convertor adapter**) are perfect for the train. These offer wingtips for an excellent fit and microphone for hands free calling. The Studio 2.0 Over-Ear headphones are a much larger device and undoubtedly bulkier to carry. These are perfect for longer journeys, particularly for when flying, as the active noise cancelling feature blocks out a good proportion of the engine noise that an aircraft generates.

PowerGen 14000mAh External Battery Pack: An essential device to carry for when battery power is low as the in-build micro USB cable will charge a multitude of devices quickly. Having an in-built lightning cable would have be good, though I have since bought a short 50cm lightning cable to accompany this device

Anything else? Inevitably, there are there are a range of peripherals that can accompany any day depending its context. I have owned a **Logitech Wireless Presenter** since beginning my teaching practice in 2005 and it still works without any problems today. **Thunderbolt to HDMI/VGA adaptors** are useful when presenting from the Air, whilst **Lightning to HDMI/VGA adaptors** complete the set for the iPad or iPhone. My **Amazon Kindle Paperwhite 6"** is the perfect companion for any longer journey and **SanDisk's 128gb Cruzer Blade** is my USB flash drive of course.

Whilst I do very much consider myself a digital native, there are times when I yearn to be a digital immigrant, viewing the technological landscape with a more critical eye. That said, it is not uncommon for me to undergo a self-imposed digital detox whilst on annual leave, going as far as signing out of social media and deleting several apps on my mobile and tablet devices. There is much to be said for viewing the world through ones' own eyes rather than through a social media news feed or a camera lens. Much like in 1999, where there was no hashtag to accompany the evening at Wembley Arena that I referred to earlier in this piece.

Oh, and for those might have been wondering, the acts performing that evening were Heaven 17, Bananarama, Culture Club and Belinda Carlisle!

@Darcy1968   Darcy Moore

Learner, reader, educator, deputy principal, English teacher, photographer, genealogist & blogger currently in New Delhi, India #citizenscience #BigHistory #DNA. Kiama, Australia

Thinking back over the last five years about tech tools that have been in my bag or pocket there are some proven stayers and some other, more recent essentials that make my life connected, pleasant and productive.

Hardware
My MacBook Pro (Retina, 15-inch, late 2013) 2.6 GHz Intel Core i7 comes most places with me and is indispensable to my jobs as a deputy principal, university lecturer and teacher but is also fundamental to photography and travelling. A Chrome browser and the Apple email client are the most used tools on the laptop and sometimes I forget how important Skype and Sonos[77] are to my week. My iPhone 6 with Mophie Juice Pack Plus[78] is ever-present and when I am travelling uber-light, a Jorno bluetooth keyboard[79] turns it into a typewriter when connected to my Ulysses app[80].

My Kindle Paperwhite (7th Generation) is with me on the train each day and last thing at night. The ability to swipe my finger and curate quotes and notes is fundamental for my blogging and other writing. My Kindle Highlights page is a record of what has stimulated rather than sticky notes or dog-eared pages that cannot be accessed from anywhere.

A Fitbit Flex[81] provides data about sleeping patterns, activity and weight (as it is connected to Aria scales[82]). I have never made the time to enter food consumed but wish I did.

Social Media
Although Twitter has changed dramatically, for the worse, in recent years it has been my favourite social media since early 2008. I can imagine life without it but would be sad if that happened. Facebook, for all the issues that come along with its "one portal to rule them all" philosophy, is an incredible tool. There are several important professional groups that bring us together as teachers, sharing resources, ideas and laughs. Yammer is great for staying in contact with colleagues in the NSW Department of Education and also other Big History teachers[83].

---

[77] Sonos. https://www.sonos.com/en-au/home

[78] Morphie Juice Pack Plus. http://www.mophie.com/shop/juice-pack-plus-iphone-6

[79] Jorno bluetooth keyboard. https://jornostore.com/

[80] Ulysses app. http://www.darcymoore.net/2016/04/18/workflow-ulysses

[81] Fitbit Flex. https://www.fitbit.com/au/flex

[82] Aria scales. https://www.fitbit.com/au/aria

Photography

Flickr is a longtime favourite for photo storage and sharing and I use Alan Levine's great Flickr CC[84] tool for inserting images directly into my blog. Adobe Lightroom CC with Topaz plugins are essential tools on my MacBook Pro. Shots taken with my Nikon D700 or D800 are uploaded to Lightroom using Cardette Ultra[85].

Increasingly I am experimenting with mobile Lightroom[86] and a host of mobile Adobe apps. I use Camera+ for zooming shots on my phone. Snapseed is a good all-round phone editing app and Distressed[87] is another favourite for editing. Eyeem[88] is greatly preferred for sharing images over Instagram. Just add a Joby Gorillapod with Olloclip Studio to my phone and I have a powerful mobile video or photography kit. Shots taken with my Nikon D700 or D800 are uploaded to Lightroom using Cardette Ultra.

Apps for school and University

GAFE, especially Google Classroom[89], is now my main sharing tools with students at school. I also use the education version of Weebly for student websites. Adobe Spark is a really great suite of apps for the classroom that allow students to make images, video and web pages easily. Edmodo is still my favourite app for sharing with my university students. The Australian Macquarie Dictionary app is used most days. My Leef iBridge[90] is a great USB which connects to iOS devices and to a regular USB port.

Other tools

Weatherzone+ is probably more important than I give it credence. Flashlight is super handy when the lights are out or one is walking home late through the wetlands that surround my home. 1Password manages all my password security needs across my iPhone, MacBook and iPad. The Audible app is used every day as I walk to listen to audiobooks. Feedly houses my RSS feeds.

What do you have in your bag and pockets?

---

[83] Big History. *https://school.bighistoryproject.com/*

[84] Alan Levine's Flickr CC tool. *http://cogdog.github.io/flickr-cc-helper/*

[85] Cardette Ultra. *http://www.moshi.com/peripheral-card-reader-cardette-usb-3*

[86] Mobile Lightroom. *https://helpx.adobe.com/lightroom/how-to/lightroom-mobile.html*

[87] Distressed. *https://itunes.apple.com/au/app/distressed-fx/id585702631?mt=8*

[88] Eyeem. *https://www.eyeem.com/u/darcy1968*

[89] Google Classroom. *https://classroom.google.com/*

[90] Leef iBridge. *http://www.leefco.com/ibridge*

@mhawksey   Martin Hawksey

Innovation, Community & Technology Officer @A_L_T | Google Expert apps Script | Interested in Open Education, EdTech, Mashups, Analytics, Data, Networks

In June 2014, I was given a wearable, the Samsung Gear Live smartwatch. Back then I certainly didn't imagine writing about wearables as one of my #EdTechRations. It's not that I couldn't see the potential of wearables in education, something featured in the 2013 NMC's Horizon Report[91], the ability to integrate technology as part of your everyday life opens the potential for discrete interactions, contextual information, logging and more.

The issue I had with my Samsung Gear Live was integration in my day-to-day life. With a one day battery lifespan and the need for plug-in charging most mornings, the watch was left at my bedside, completely flat. The turning point was receiving a second smartwatch, the Moto 360[92]. Like the Gear Live, the Moto 360 also uses the Android Wear operating system. What was the difference that makes wearables part of my everyday life? Wireless charging. The ability to place my watch on a dock beside my bed in the safe knowledge that, by morning, it would be full charged. That added a level of convenience that overcame another issue with wearables, the aesthetic ... would you wear it?

My Moto 360 is the bottom of the line model and, on appearance, you can tell. Whilst the watch's physical design and finish is underwhelming I have been able to personalise it to try and overcome some of its shortcomings. Whilst I could have changed the strap I didn't think that would help much so instead I forked out £1.39 on the WatchMaker Premium app. This app lets you install, remix and create your own watch faces. I have written about 'becoming a watchmaker'[93] and shared some other designs[94]. My current favourite watch face is a remix of a Star Trek inspired face which I've tweaked by adding the date and calendar information.

The inclusion of features like calendar information is one of the key reasons I use smartwatches; the convenience of an easily accessible awareness mechanism that allows with the minimum of effort access to notifications I find useful beyond just the time. If the creators of the Android Wear platform, the operating system used on my smartwatches, read that I'm sure their hearts would sink as their ambition was for it to be more than just some text.

---

[91] NMC Horizon Report, 2013 - *http://www.nmc.org/pdf/2013-horizon-report-HE.pdf*

[92] Moto 360 - *https://www.motorola.com/us/products/moto-360*

[93] Becoming a watch maker - *https://mashe.hawksey.info/2015/05/becoming-a-watch-maker/*

[94] Drawing squircles in Lau for WatchMaker (using WatchMaker functions) - *https://mashe.hawksey.info/2015/07/drawing-squircles-in-lau-for-watchmaker-using-watchmaker-functions/*

LCARS Round - Original

LCARS Round - Custom

Android Wear, like other smartwatch operating systems, creates a platform for rich notifications that can integrate with actions, include visual cues and assist with immediate consumption. I do however occasionally use some of the other actions available. The challenge is on such as small touch interface understanding user input. This was highlighted in a 2015 session at Google's developer conference Google I/O[95] in which several projects were announced to address the issues of wearable devices. Highlighting the 1954 research by Fitts[96], the smallest screen size that can comfortably be used for human interaction is around the size or most current smartwatches.

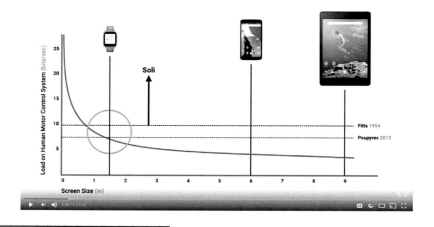

---

[95] Google I/O 2015 - A little badass. Beautiful. Tech and human. Work and love. ATAP - *https://youtu.be/mpbWQbkl8_g?t=9m16s*

[96] The information capacity of the human motor system in controlling the amplitude of movement - *http://sing.stanford.edu/cs303-sp11/papers/1954-Fitts.pdf*

Solutions announced in the Google session included:

- Soli[97], a miniature radar chip that can fit into devices like smartwatches that can be used to detect touchless interactions; and
- Jacquard[98], which enables touch capabilities to be woven into fabrics. Another interface that has been bubbling around for years but now having its moment is voice interaction.

If, like me, you experimented with voice interfaces over a decade ago and feeling disappointed it's easy to think these are still clunky and unresponsive. Competition from Apple Siri, Amazon Alexa and Google Assistant has resulted in systems that are increasingly able to not only understand words but also use other factors such as context to interpret intent. Voice driven actions are already a feature of Android Wear and the next version of the operating system is set to get an enhancement with Google Assistant.

The devices you wear and being comfortable in talking to, particularly in public, again underline the personal buy-in required for wearables. Within a learning context I struggle to see a time where you can assume a group of students will all have the same wearable device or even all using the same wearable platform such as Android Wear. If advocating wearables in education privacy should be a primary concern. Wearables are often the slave to a master such as your Android or Apple mobile; or a cloud based service like Fitbit. As such they can collect a whole host of sensitive data. For example, researchers have already used sensor data from smartwatches to predict with a degree of accuracy a PIN you enter at a cash machine[99].

Which leaves me with the question, having bought into wearables have I already sold out?

---

[97] Soli - *https://atap.google.com/soli/*

[98] Jacquard - *https://atap.google.com/jacquard/*

[99] Friend or Foe?: Your Wearable Devices Reveal Your Personal PIN - *https://doi.org/10.1145/2897845.2897847*

@mattlingard   **Matt Lingard**

Learning   Technologist,   Head   of *@UWLTEL @UniWestLondon,*   SFHEA, *@A_L_T* Trustee, *@UKHeLF*. London, UK

I don't consider myself an early adopter of technologies or gadgets but it's all relative I suppose. I got my first smartphone in 2011, ahead of many I imagine, but a long time after many of my EdTech colleagues. After dissing the iPad in a Future of Technology in Education conference keynote (*#FOTE10*[100]) I saw the light and bought my first tablet in 2012.

Wearables
I don't own any wearable digital technologies, just a regular watch, which I do check regularly. I still find myself checking my watch for the time when I've got my phone in my hand even though a small eye movement to the top right of my screen would do the same job!

In my pocket
I always have my phone with me, in my pocket when it's not in my hand. For work I usually wear a jacket but if not, my phone will be in a trouser pocket. It seems I've never learned the lesson from my first smartphone - day 2, back pocket. Cracked screen.

I'm on my third smartphone now. For the record: Samsung Galaxy S II, HTC One Mini and currently a Sony Xperia Z3 Compact. I can't say one has been particularly better than the others. They've all done what I needed them too. Having said that they have all had problems, albeit mainly user error: cracked screen (the Samsung), overheating battery killer (the HTC), and smashed screen & rear glass cover (Sony). I have finally seen sense and bought a protective cover.

I've opted for slightly smaller phones recently (the Mini and the Compact) partly because I prefer the 'pocketability' of them, but primarily to minimise repetitive strain injury (RSI). It's something I used to suffer from when using a mouse, which has been solved by a sideways mouse and smaller keyboard. However, when I started using my first smartphone regularly my neck pains returned. In part this seemed to be due to stretching my thumb across the screen, so I stick with narrower phones. That doesn't solve it completely, I still have to be careful about overuse.

I use my phone throughout the day; primarily for the Internet, much less for texting and calls. I don't take many photos but my phone has pretty much replaced my 'real' camera these days.

In my bag

---

[100] Future of Technology in Education. *http://fote-conference.com/*

I have an Android tablet (currently a Samsung Galaxy Tab S) which I carry to-and-from work each day. I take it to meetings but still prefer to make notes and write actions in a notebook with a pen. I use my tablet a lot during my one and a quarter hour commute, which includes a 45-minute tube journey. In the morning, I mainly use it to read the Guardian. I subscribe to the Guardian & Observer Tablet Edition as I like to have the limited, collated content of the 'real' paper rather than the almost unlimited content of the online Guardian. In the evening, it's the Kindle app and sometimes iPlayer or All4 (Channel 4) downloads. I've tried and failed with Podcasts many times; my mind wanders too much. I do quite a bit of note making during my commute, sometimes on my tablet but often on my phone.

This article has been written on my phone during several tube journeys.

Also in my bag is a Ravpower portable charger[101] but that's it for technology, unless an umbrella counts.

Apps
I use a variety of apps on both devices but in particular: Twitter, Dropbox (and OneDrive for Business), Evernote (sporadically), Remember the Milk (religiously) and my favourite, Google Maps. I use it for directions of course, but often just to browse. I love maps.

A special mention must go to Twitter. I use it a lot, tweeting less so recently although still regularly. But I follow it a lot and it is my only significant social network. I mainly use it professionally and it has been incredibly important in my personal development and I'd go as far to say, my career.

For most of the year I remain fully connected but twice a year I do go completely offline, from work at least. I switch off email (I actually delete my work account) and Twitter. Only non-work content survives and that's pretty much limited to the Guardian & the BBC, while some holiday apps kick-in too, particularly TripAdvisor.

So, that's me for technology on the go. Quite limited in gadgets; mainstream in content and apps but permanently connected, for 47-weeks of the year at least.

---

[101] Ravpower Portable Charger: *http://www.ravpower.com/external-batteries.html*

@ryantracey   **Ryan Tracey**

E-Learning Provocateur. Sydney, Australia

I have always considered it quite curious that as an "e-learning" specialist, I've never been one to blindly follow tech trends. I never felt the urge to buy a Google Glass nor an Apple Watch, for example. And while I enjoy video games as much as the next guy, I'm not inclined to play them 24/7. For me, the role of technology is to meet a need – not vice versa. So, my general approach to gadgetry is *less is more*... until I need more. Below is an overview of the ones I currently need.

Smartphone: More than just a telephone, this little device gives me immediate access to the Internet. I can Google something at a whim, translate a foreign word, jot down a thought on OneNote, participate on Twitter, and employ a range of other handy apps. In addition, I use the camera (still and video) for "authentic" content production, and while I claim to not blindly follow tech trends, I feel it's important to at least see what all the fuss is about with popular pastimes such as Pokémon Go.

Tablet: Actually I could quite easily live without this, but my target audience can't. So I must ensure that my work is compatible with this device.

Laptop: Some people argue that tablets are designed for consumption while laptops and desktops are more suitable for production, while other people recoil in horror at such a notion. I happen to agree with it, so I insist on using a laptop. At home I've replaced my desktop with a laptop for its portability.

Recharge cords: I've learned the hard way that you need multiple cords strategically located where you use your devices most often, such as at home and in the office. I'm always pleased when I see a recharge kiosk at a conference venue; it's a nice touch.

VR headset: I'm a big advocate of experimenting with emerging technologies, even if (*especially* if) it seems beyond the grasp of mere mortals. Virtual Reality falls into this bucket, and while a non-coder like me is unlikely to ever build a full-blown immersion on Unity, I can easily take 360˚ photos and videos and experience them on a $20 Google Cardboard[102]. I've recently upgraded to a Gear VR[103] headset, and I'm excited by the introduction of collapsible pocket VR viewers to the market.

Xbox: As mentioned, I'm no gamer, but I feel it's important to keep abreast of the latest advances in the trailblazing video game industry. Besides, it's a bit of fun, and it continually reminds me of the engagement value of game-based learning.

---

[102] Google Cardboard - *https://vr.google.com/cardboard/*

[103] Gear VR - *https://www.oculus.com/gear-vr/*

PC headset: I own an old Sennheiser headset that I protect like a jealous lover. It has a USB connection which means that it is always recognised as soon as it's plugged in, and its recordings are crystal clear. I use this headset to participate in webinars and when working with software such as Audacity.

Earbuds: I always keep a pair of these handy, as I don't know when I might need them. Whether it's to block out my colleagues in the open plan office, or to play media on public transport without being a douche, they're easy to whip out at a moment's notice. I own a pair that wind around a little plastic disc to keep the cord untangled, and I've also invested in a pair of Bose noise-cancelling earphones in case of emergency.

Opal card: Equivalent to the Oyster card in London, the Opal card swipes me onto buses, trains and ferries all over Sydney. Gone are the days of carrying a pocketful of change or queuing up for a weekly pass, every week. Good riddance!

Credit card: In the same vein as the Opal card, I love how my credit card allows me to make purchases free of the burden of hard currency. apps such as 'Beat The Q'[104] that link up to my card are similarly convenient. I also find comfort in the knowledge that if I need to pay for something urgently (for example, a taxi fare), I can.

Google Cast[105]: Circling back to my smartphone, I'm delighted to stream movies and music to my TV without having to boot up my computer. I've since dispensed with my old-fashioned stereo system, and I find myself enjoying more MOOCs and TED talks on the big screen.

---

[104] Beat the Q - *https://www.beattheq.com/*

[105] Google Cast - *https://www.google.com/cast/*

@JaneBozarth   Jane Bozarth

World's Oldest Millennial, Author: Show Your Work (Working Out Loud) & more, Positive Deviant, Doctor of Learnin' Stuff 919.789.1611. Warning: WYSIWYG. North Carolina, USA

For years I kept a little pocket-sized spiral notebook handy for jotting down book titles when they crossed my path, in reading or in conversation or when spotted in an airport bookshop or whatnot. Then when I'd go to the library I'd pull the most recent books out into a pile and sort through to decide which I wanted to check out. One day in maybe 2000-ish I went into the library and realized I'd left my notebook on my desk at home. I remember thinking: "I wish there was a place online where I could store the titles I wanted to read, and then just somehow access that when I was at the library."

Guess what? Turns out the library already had that: an online card catalogue with user account-specific features that did exactly what I wanted.

And guess what else? The lesson I learned that day was: If you hear yourself saying "I wish there was a tool that _____", odds are there is. I found the library moment happening time and time again, when I said: "I wish there was something that would send an alert when there's a traffic jam to or from the office. I wish I could find out what is the name of that song they're playing in the shoe store. I wish there was somewhere I could just store my music online and access it from anywhere on any device." Well, I have all that now, and so much more. Some days it's like rubbing a magic lamp: wish, and it appears.

The advent of the smartphone changed my life, of course. No more notebooks, and I had a device always with me and never left home on my desk. While I'm usually on my phone, most apps work on my iPad, too, and many of them even on my desktop, so I can access whatever I need wherever I am.

My favourites?
For daily use, I rely heavily on social tools, especially Facebook and Twitter. This is where my friends are, and where most non-office business conversations begin. It keeps me connected to my community and alerts me to breaking news.

World Time Buddy[106]: 20 years of schooling and I still can't figure out time zones. World Time Buddy lets me input several cities – say, Sydney, Chicago, and London – gives me parallel timelines for each. Easy-squeezy to find a time for a call.

Alexa (Amazon Echo)[107]: I say it at home, it's on my phone shopping list when I get to the store. It sets timers. It plays songs on demand. It never gets tired of

---

[106] World Time Buddy - *http://www.worldtimebuddy.com/*

[107] Amazon Alexa - *https://www.amazon.co.uk/dp/B01GAGVIE4/*

telling my husband that the Colts won Superbowl XLI. It knows the meaning of life is 42. It knows what the fox says. And it tells jokes.

IF (If This Then That)[108]:   IF connects different social accounts via "recipes" created and shared by users. My favourites at the moment: Every link I post to Facebook is synced to an Evernote notebook, making it searchable later. Every photo I post to Instagram is also saved to Dropbox. I use Alexa timers for cooking; these are synced to my phone via IF in case I'm out on the deck or in the yard. It'll work with smart home devices like Nest thermostats. You can link to email, too, like getting a notification every time the President signs a new law or Amazon adds new free eBooks.

For traveling—which sometimes feels like a daily event – I depend on all those emergency rations plus a few more:

Google Maps: GPS has improved exponentially since the early days. My navigation app of choice is Google Maps, which I find gives me the information in the way I want it. This quite literally saved my life one night when, in a strange city, I began having an allergic reaction to something I'd eaten and was able to find a pharmacy only steps away.

TripIt[109]: Stores trip itineraries and confirmation numbers via emails I forward from airlines and hotels and such. Sends texts reminding me to check in and get a boarding pass. Alerts me to gate changes and flight delays. And twice in the last year TripIt has sent notification that there'd been a drop in the price I paid for a plane ticket: I contacted the airlines and got an adjustment to the fee.

GateGuru[110]: Guides to most airports with location of restaurants and amenities by terminal/gate, and user ratings for food and things like Wi-Fi.

Other? **Google Translate**, which uses your phone's camera to read signs, menus, and even handwritten notes. Transportation apps like Tube Exits[111] that not only offer subway journey planners but also alternatives, icons showing which stations have only steps, and advice for which car to enter that will put you closest to the station exit when you arrive.

It's how my life runs. Of course, your life will have different requirements, and you'll likely find other things that meet your own specific requirements. The great thing is there are so many tools to choose from - I love living in the future.

Confession, though - I am sorry I didn't keep those notebooks!

---

[108] IFTTT - *https://ifttt.com/*

[109] TripIt - *https://www.tripit.com/*

[110] GateGuru - *http://www.gateguru.com/*

[111] Tube Exits - *http://www.tubeexits.co.uk/*

@sarahknight   **Sarah Knight**

Senior co-design manager, Student Experience, JISC. UK

My uses of technology are from the perspective of a working mother who balances the role of being a Senior Co design manager at Jisc for 4 days a week and being a mother to three school-age young boys! For me technology supports me with managing these two roles and enables me also to maintain and keep in touch with friends and family as well as maintain my professional networks.

As I am currently working on the JISC Building digital capability project[112], I have applied my #EdTechRations to the 6 elements of the digital capability framework (Helen Betham[113]). The framework describes six overlapping elements of digital capability for staff and students. I was keen to see how the technology I use is also enabling me to develop my digital capabilities which is an important aspect of my professional role working for JISC.

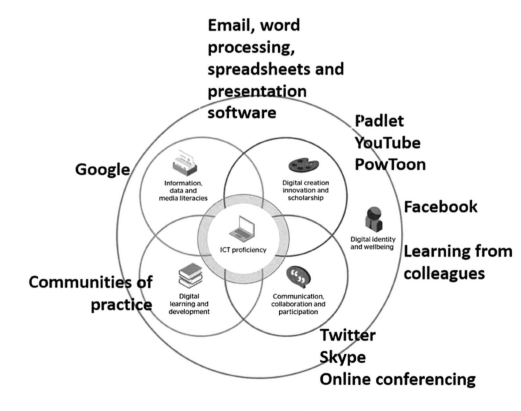

Email, word processing, spreadsheets and presentation software

Google

Information, data and media literacies

Digital creation innovation and scholarship

ICT proficiency

Digital learning and development

Communication, collaboration and participation

Digital identity and wellbeing

Padlet YouTube PowToon

Facebook

Learning from colleagues

Communities of practice

Twitter Skype Online conferencing

---

[112] JISC Building Digital Capability - *https://www.jisc.ac.uk/rd/projects/building-digital-capability*

[113] 6 elements of the digital capability framework - *http://repository.jisc.ac.uk/6239/1/Digital_capabilities_six_elements.pdf*

ICT proficiency

My use of technology has evolved over the past few years both for my work and for what I use in my personal life, to reflect the advances of digital. Although the most important device I use for my work is still my laptop and a Wi-Fi connection, my smartphone is a tool which I increasingly use for work too. We are now permanently connected to the internet through free Wi-Fi in cafes, on trains and even buses, this makes working on the move far more of a reality that it was a few years ago. I use my internet-connected laptop and phone at home, on trains or in the office, on a daily basis for my work, to communicate, interact and work with my colleagues, with project teams and with staff in colleges and universities all around the UK. My essential tools and *#EdTechRations* **for work are email, word processing, spreadsheets and presentation software** which fulfil the minimum requirements in terms of ICT proficiency.

Information, data and media literacy

The easy access to information and data though the web, and utilising search engines like **Google, another of my *#EdTechRations***, is something we take for granted now. To be able to access information in textual, visual or multimedia format on whatever topic we need, is seamless now. Whether it be live updates on the weather forecast or train departure information, access to online learning materials to support my children's learning to viewing TED Talk videos of international experts. It's all there for us to harness. Increasingly data manipulation and interrogation skills are becoming essential, in order to maximise the value and power that the data can offer.

The importance of being able to critically assess information and media sources has been brought into focus over the past few months with the changing political landscape and this is an area which everyone needs to play a responsible role as good digital citizens.

Digital communication, collaboration and participation

As I am home based for part of my working week, I use Skype and Skype for Business to connect and communicate with team members. This is an effective way of managing meetings and ensuring we make the best use of everyone's valuable time. This saves travel time and costs and is something I could not do my job without. So, **Skype is an essential *#EdTechRation*** for me.

Having worked on numerous international online conferences from 2005, I value the role of online conferencing tools to support collaboration and online participation. Online webinars can bring together students and staff from across the world in a vibrant and participatory environment. Building confidence to participate in such an environment is important to ensure that everyone gets the most from their experience and feels able to contribute in a meaningful way.

Professionally I find Twitter an essential way of maintaining my professional networks and keeping up to date. It's also offers a way of sharing effective practice, building on ideas and encouraging collaborations. The success of *#LearningWheel* as a model for digital pedagogy from Deborah Millar

(@DebKellsey) shows the power of Twitter for enabling collaborations of educators across the UK and globally. **Twitter is one #EdTechRation** I could not be without.

Digital creation, innovation and scholarship

I enjoy the range of opportunities technology offers in enabling creativity. The use of animation tools, like PowToon[114] for example, offers an easy way to create short clips. YouTube offers a platform to share digital resources easily and widely. Through my work, I have managed the creation of numerous video case studies which can be used to inspire others and share the visions staff and students have for digital. Whether it be through video, animation, visualisations – technology offers us many different lenses to share information and ideas. For me, I enjoy the challenge of learning to use new tools which I can use to develop new resources. Digital facilitates collaboration and engagement. **Padlet is one of my #EdTechRations** as this offers an easy and accessible way for participants to share ideas and engage in discussions – replacing the tried and trusted post-it notes. This has saved me many a train journey home after a workshop typing up endless post-its!

Digital learning and personal/professional development

In my current role, I am aware of the importance of modelling good practice in TEL. I believe it's important to have the opportunities of being an online student and participating in an online course, to have an empathy and understanding of what our students' experience. I was fortunate to have the opportunity of participating in a course which I was involved in its development, a SEDA accredited Institutional Change Leaders award[115] as part of the Change Agents' Network[116]. This course was delivered online in Moodle and I was required to create an e-portfolio of evidence on student/staff partnerships using Mahara. I was new to using Mahara and through its use, I realised the benefits that e-portfolio's offer. I also experienced the challenges many online learners face of fitting learning into your life when you have other roles and responsibilities. The support provided by our tutors and having peer-support was essential in motivating me to successfully complete the course.

I was also encouraged by my colleagues to set up my own blog. Although I blog in my professional capacity, I value the opportunity of sharing my own insights[117] and reflections on technology enhanced learning. Through membership of mailing lists, I keep connected with colleagues in higher and further education and follow discussions on current issues or challenges in technology enhanced learning.

---

[114] PowToon - *https://www.powtoon.com/*

[115] SEDA Change Leaders Award - *https://can.jiscinvolve.org/wp/change-leader-award/*

[116] JISC Change Agents' Network - *https://can.jiscinvolve.org/*

[117] Sarah Knight - *https://sarahknightblog.wordpress.com/*

So, **my *#EdTechRation* here is communities of practice** – peers and colleagues who can support, guide and mentor you on your professional development.

Digital identity and wellbeing

I try and maintain boundaries between my personal and professional digital identity. For me Twitter is linked to my professional identity while I use Facebook to connect on a personal level with friends and family. There is some blurring of these boundaries as many of my friends I know professionally too. Facebook allows me to keep in touch with friends and family across the world as well as keep connected to key information relating to my sons' school activities. Its allowed me to maintain relationships from my school days which without technology would not be possible in our busy day to day lives. I love the ability to share photos and to have a record or a personal diary of significant moments in my and my family's lives. **Facebook is a personal *#EdTechRation*.**

Digital safety is something of paramount importance to me. With 3 young children, I am acutely aware of the dangers they could face in the online world. As e-safety governor for their school, I play an active role in promoting the importance of staying safe online and maintaining a healthy digital presence both for children and for parents. We all have a responsibility to protect our digital wellbeing and to take control of how and when we use technology professionally and personally. Helen Beetham's blog on What is digital wellbeing[118] is an essential read on this topic and my ***#EdTechRation* here is learning from colleagues** and how technology facilitates this, as indeed this ***#EdTechRations* book** is doing.

---

[118] What is digital wellbeing? - *http://design-4-learning.blogspot.co.uk/2016/03/what-is-digital-wellbeing.html*

@lindacq   Linda Castañeda

EdTechnologist. Prof. Fac. d Educación. Universidad de Murcia (Spain). Grupo de Inv. d Tecnología Educativa GITE. Dpto DOE. Omnívora, Talkative & Learnative. Murcia, España

To think of the basic technological kit of survival for a person that loves to learn as I do (I like to define myself as talkative and 'learnative'), is trying to explain what is the most logistic part of my Personal Learning Environment (PLE). Thanks to this, I can satisfy my enthusiasm, curiosity, fears and day-to-day needs, everywhere... anytime.

Core Devices
Quevedo (a writer from The Spanish Gold Century) wrote something similar to "Once there was a man stuck to a nose" ... well, I must say: once there was a lady (me) stuck to a mobile phone.

My phone is the centre of my technological activity. It is the first screen I see every morning (even when my eyes are not open enough yet), and the last device I read every night. My phone is my camera, recorder, agenda, personal assistant, map, dictionary, translator, archive, bank office, radio, music provider and writer. If you receive any written message from me, remember that the most probable is that I have not written it, how it is well written is because of the exceptional pedagogical expertise of my Siri, that is who is writing (yes I think on Siri as a "Whom").

I always have my mobile phone with me. But close to this, is my iPad.

Since I got my first iPad (yes, the 1), it became my best notebook, drawing block and reading tool. I have changed it twice, and with the advances in the last version (basically the multitasking possibilities) It became the best device for supporting me in a working meeting.

The crucial third part of my *#EdTechRations* is my laptop. Even when I have a computer on my office or home desk, I always carry on using my laptop. It is the central device for my work and for my life too. I think I can survive (and I can make my family survive) anywhere with my laptop and an Internet connection. "Everything is there, and I can do whatever with it" (yes, I know that it is not very realistic, but I feel like that).

These three devices go almost everywhere with me. Which of them could remain at home? It depends on how big the bag I carry is; the minimum is a mobile with some accessories (smaller bags are not for me, sorry), and the best option always is my purple backpack.

Evidently, those devices are not as useful as they are without the proper software inside. I am not a computer scientist, so I have just criteria related to usability to choose software, therefore, this is my selection:

Core Software:
On this selection I will include ONLY the software that is critical for me and, therefore, is installed on these three devices, even when some of those tools are more useful in some of them than in other.

One of my best friends and colleagues says that I am a Web-lady, and absolutely, I am. I need a browser to survive. Give me a browser, and I will see the world.

I definitely need Twitter nowadays to survive; this is clearly my best information source and the core of my Personal Learning Network (PLN), what is in fact, the heart of my PLE. I love to say that thanks to Twitter I have an eye on the shoulder of my favourite people around the world. Teachers, academics, influencers, journalists, critics, practitioners... some of them have become my friends, but all they are there, and thanks to Twitter I can see their enthusiasms from very close. I believe that being on Twitter since 2007, I have seen from a privileged position, some of the most exciting changes and evolutions in the thought and use of Educational Technology in the last decade.

I think the second most critical part of the software I use is Dropbox. More than the virtual space that I have there, the way in which this tool is synchronised in all my devices and how I can access to everything everywhere is fantastic. This is my personal archive, available anywhere; not just for archiving, but also searching, and sharing. It is having everything stored on more than just my computer or home backups. I confess that I do not use its possibilities for synchronically collaborating with others, but for everything else, I use it.

I have a very close connection to the Google tools. Google engine is THE tool, but Google Calendar regulates my life. Apart from including every event in my life (and alarms for everything!), I share calendars with a lot of people; my husband, my group of research, the associations I participate. I feel that thanks to this (and its synchronisation with the whole devices of my life), I can use my own memory (that is very very scarce) to manage other important things.

Apart from those two, to socially survive I need at least an email client and an instant message tool. Depending on the networks and the personal moment I have tried different ones, but I always need them.

The next tool of my life from the Google universe is Drive. I use it very much for creating documents (spreadsheets, slideshows, text documents) with other people, but also for creating a document just to myself. I usually use a local productivity suite on my laptop and desktop computer, BUT I feel more committed to the use of GDrive because I can delocalize my documents and advance on them from everywhere...

For reading and manage my information sources, I use Sente[119]. It is one of the most critical tools that I have in my academic work; I use it to read papers and manage my references but also to take notes, tag documents and organise authors. Even though it hasn't changed or developed over the last few years, I continue using it because of its incredible possibilities for sharing libraries with other people. I hope it is rejuvenated soon... but unfortunately, it is just a hope.

YouTube is an excellent tool for me. I use it to watch videos about everything, to publish my videos to my students and family, to organise videos that I love to share. Therefore, YouTube is a tool that helps me to support the three parts of my PLE (information source, reflection/creation tool, and sharing space).

I use blogs to maintain a public online record about my work in accessible spaces. So, for this and for every online public site that I need to create, I use WordPress.

Other tools that I have close to me
I love to carry close to me Spotify to get my music everywhere. And I use Google

---

[119] Sente - *http://www.thirdstreetsoftware.com/*

Maps to localise myself in the world.

Google translator[120] is my reading helper, and it saves me from my habit to create new words in other languages. The Spanish Real Academia App is one of my favourites, as well (yes, I also destroy my mother tongue), I use WordReference[121] for the language uses.

I like the possibilities of Augmented Reality, so I always have a QR Code reader on my phone. Recognising star names is one of my favourite hobbies on quiet nights, but my knowledge about the sky is not too good, so I love SkyGuide[122] for looking at the sky in an augmented way.

I publish pictures on Instagram and Flickr. Instagram serves to interchange some personal info about our life with my friends (I am NOT on Facebook).

Crucial Technological Accessories
To be sure that my devices will be as useful as I expect all the time, I carry some essential accessories:

- **Battery banks.** The size of them depends on the size of the bag I can carry.
- **USB memory** stick(s)
- **Charging Cables:** the minimum is a lighting charger and a mini USB charger with a two USB plug. The optimal includes a socket bank that allows me to survive to the only one plug rooms.
- **Connection cables:** the minimum: headphones and adapter from lighting to VGA, the optimal, everything I need to connect my devices with everything.

Other Critical Accessories:
I cannot say that these are part of my PLE, may be they're too superficial, but definitely I appreciate having these with me to be more comfortable, and being physically comfortable is crucial to better learning. So, I almost always carry: a Spanish fan, a mini umbrella and my sunglasses. A note-book and a fountain pen with cartridges to recharge it. My essential medicines, some old hotel room cards (to leave the rooms to maintain the electricity for charging my devices, even if I am not in the room), tissues, chewing gum, perfume, hands cream, lip balm and a toothbrush travel kit, complete my life in the backpack. All of them are parts of my socio-material entanglement to learn... and I love to think about myself as a learning being, so they are part of my Personal Learning Environment that is also my closer environment.

---

[120] Google Translate - *https://translate.google.co.uk/*

[121] WordReference - *http://www.wordreference.com/*

[122] SkyGuie - *http://www.fifthstarlabs.com/*

@RealGeoffBarton   Geoff Barton

Headteacher and writer of textbooks & articles about English, literacy, grammar, school leadership and assorted trivia. Suffolk, UK

In 1979, the writer Craig Raine unknowingly kick-started a new, short-lived genre which came to be known as 'Martian poetry'. It resulted from a poem he published called 'A Martian Sends a Postcard Home'[123]. It begins like this:

> Caxtons are mechanical birds with many wings
> and some are treasured for their markings –
>
> they cause the eyes to melt
> or the body to shriek without pain.
>
> I have never seen one fly, but
> sometimes they perch on the hand.

As the title tells us, this is the viewpoint of a Martian, a creature looking through alien eyes at some everyday objects that we take for granted.

The item he describes, that perches on the hand, that can melt our eyes or make us shriek painlessly, remains my most indispensable item of technology.

The clue to what it is lies in its first word. The merchant William Caxton is usually credited with bringing the printing press to England in 1476 and establishing the first bookshop.

The epoch-changing technology he unleashed all those years ago would change humans' relationships with each other, with knowledge and with our sense of the past. The new technology was, of course, the book.

We often forget, as we turn over the winged pages, laughing or crying at what the inky marks on the page convey, how radical the concept of the book was and is, and how unthinkable it would be to live without it.

There are few journeys I undertake without a book. Even my weekly visit to the supermarket has me wondering whether I should stuff a book in the car boot, just in case of breakdown (mechanical, that is, not emotional).

My obsession with books means that I am unnerved if I visit someone's house or office and there aren't books on display. Such an environment seems to me unnatural, almost soulless. Similarly, if I read a newspaper or magazine article

---

[123] Craig Raine, 'A Martian Sends a Postcard Home' -
http://www.poetrybyheart.org.uk/poems/a-martian-sends-a-postcard-home/

about someone with an illustrative photograph taken in front of a book case, then it's to the subject's books that my eye is drawn. I want to see if they read what I read, to reflect on what we may have in common, on what their choice of books reveals about them.

And if you happened to recommend a book to me and suggested I borrow your copy, you'd receive a polite 'no thanks' from me. I'll then buy my own copy because reading for me is always a physical act. I underline, I make margin notes, I scribble quotations in the end pages.

It's why I was so pleased that Apple called their laptops 'MacBooks'. In doing so they played to my narrative that books and computers aren't so different. The concept of the book – a gateway to knowledge, a trusted friend, a portable companion – is at the heart of the computer I use.

I can no longer use a deskbound computer, though once that was all there was. It has to be a laptop. It has to be Apple.

I was an early convert to home computers. I used the spare cash from a stingy first year as a teacher to buy one of those Amstrad PCWs. It had a memory capacity of 256K and it printed out in an unsubtle pixelated typeface onto printer paper which you had to tear carefully apart. It had limited font size, no font choice, a crude underlining function that was badly proportioned, and no capacity for including images.

It was terrible; it was wonderful. I used that early computer to write handouts for lessons, articles, my early textbooks, and the school magazine.

Like all the computers I've since owned, it rarely got switched off.

I'm now on my seventh Apple laptop. Early on, this one needed some extra memory, and the technician fitting it said 'your computer has undergone five years of use in the six months you've had it'. It seems that I work my laptops into the dust, always having multiple programs open, always flitting between documents and applications. The computer encourages, and possibly indulges, my butterfly mind.

Much of my time I'm reading stuff. I read news and opinions, gleaning much from Twitter which has become established as my indispensable gateway to ideas both serious and frivolous. Like most people I started with the assumption that Twitter was trivial, time-wasting, a platform for the egotistical to pontificate. And sometimes it is. But I've also learnt a great deal from it, read articles and blogs that I wouldn't otherwise have seen and become connected with a huge cyber group of people with interests often similar to, and sometimes different from, mine.

What I love most is what I see as I'm writing my *#EdTechRations*. I've retreated to my usual hiding place in school – the sixth form common room. Many of the students around me also have laptops open. Their clattering punctuates the background sound of chatter and laughter.

Many of these sixth formers have done precisely what they do with pencil cases: they have customised their laptops with covers, stickers, and badges. In a sense they are doing what I do as I read a book: my markings on the page are the equivalent of their personalisation of their computers. It's how we make technology our own.

My MacBook Pro is battered and erratic. It almost wheezes as I start it up. It has begun to crash at awkward moments. I sense it hasn't much more life in it. I'm hoping it clings on till Easter, when, inevitably, a new laptop will render this one merely a memory, an old friend who's moved on.

I surprise myself to talk about a humble laptop like this. That's because it isn't just a computer. It's an ally, an enabler, a pal. And because it has 'book' at the heart of its name, there's something almost – note: almost – as personal to me about this MacBook Pro as those many mechanical birds that fill my shelves and teem across my desk.

@stipton   **Shannon Tipton**

Owner, Learning Rebels LLC. International Speaker, Blended and Micro Learning Strategist, Author, Top 100 eLearning blogger. Disrupter of Status Quo. Chicago, USA

When David approached me to write a piece about emergency rations and technology, my first thought was - what would I need if the zombie apocalypse (ZA)[124] finally hits? You know, when I'm running around calmly whilst all those around me are literally losing their minds? What tools would help my escape - I picture myself calmly gathering assorted accoutrements, when most likely I'll be running around in circles trying to find my car keys.

This leads me to think of the Tile[125] on my keychain. It is well known that I used to spend endless hours looking for keys that are always in a place where they didn't belong. Additionally, I have a Tile attached to my iPad case. I know, I could use the "find my iPad" function on my phone but the Tile app sits upfront and proud, I hit that baby and ding, ding, ding...my iPad goes off! Handy, right? Think about all the items you misplace, remotes, wallets, small children...you can find them in an instant.

With car keys in hand, I turn to Google Maps. I have been known to get lost going around the block. When the ZA hits, I want to find myself on the quickest, most direct route to wherever they are not and as a frequent traveler the apps I find are indispensable are: Uber/Lyft, Hilton, American Airlines and FlightView[126]. When running with aluminum foil on my head protecting my beautiful brain I may want to find an airport, hop a flight and grab an Uber to the nearest Hilton where I can camp out by the bar at the pool and hope for the best.

Okay, I assume David meant for me to take this seriously. All the above apps are seriously on my must have list. Of course, to have those apps work - one must have a mobile device. Where would I be without my phone and tablet, with these devices you have a mobile photo and video studio at the palm of your hand.

[124] Image source: Kevin Thorn | @learnnuggets | *http://NuggetHead.net*

[125] Tile - *https://www.thetileapp.com/*

[126] FlightView - *https://www.flightview.com/*

Literally, in the palm of your hand. Whereas, before you might have to fire up Photoshop or a video editing program on your computer to make something epic, now, it's a matter of turning on iMovie (for iPhone) or YouTube Capture[127] (device agnostic) for video, and Instagram for pictures. You know you can edit pictures in Instagram and save them in all their glory without posting, right? Super genius!

It follows then, that I can then use this video journal to send to those searching for a place to hide where they can join me at the swim up bar at the Hilton. Here's the thing, when the ZA eats up the interwebs, then what? ARGGGG - hair pulling and teeth gnashing! We then must depend on each other. We will need to connect on a human level. This makes me think about my network and connections and the hope that I have been diligent in strengthening those connections. You never know where in the world you will have to go and who's knowledge and couch you will need to survive.

In other words, to survive one must prepare. My preparations to survive would include:

Twitter. I know, I can hear the collective groan as you read this. Some "don't get it" and you don't have to - but let me tell you this...when you need up to the moment news, that's where I go. Most likely there will be a hashtag dedicated to the ZA such as *#ZombieHoards* or *#ProtectYourBrains* that we all can follow and get critical information. You never know, there may be a backchannel to follow and we can discover their plans... *#ZombieConference2017*. Believe me, if I want news about the latest hoard of zombies, I'm hoping someone at twitter is still feeding the stream.

Slack. I have many Slack groups, each dedicated to a specific idea. One, for all my techie friends, another for friends who can give me content feedback, another dedicated to a book club...you get the picture. My Slack groups have saved me more than once, and in the event of a ZA, I would hope that we could depend on each other in a good way - not the Lord of the Flies way.

WordPress. Seems like an odd choice I know. However, within WordPress I'll be able to document my findings. Stay away from Chicago! Go to San Diego! Blogging is not only for capturing and sharing thoughts of the moment, but also for transparency. Using a blog to keep the team updated, to post project plans, to collaborate on documents and checklists. Perhaps one group of survivors has made their way to Miami and another to San Francisco - how can they connect and share the best way to to make a cappuccino? Through a blog!

YouTube Capture. I mentioned this earlier - but when it comes to developing short burst pieces of valuable information, YouTube Capture is the way to go. As an app on your mobile device you can take video, upload to YouTube and then quickly edit. This allows you to share the best practices for breaking into your

---

[127] YouTube Capture - *https://www.youtube.com/capture*

local Walmart and getting supplies to last out the year. As with other micro-learning methods, perfection is not needed, it's all about the "just-in-time" support. Build your YouTube channel and share your work. Save mankind.

Evernote: Then there was one. One app to rule them all...Evernote does it all. You can share, collaborate, store, curate. All the things needed to share and store important information while running from the Zombie hoards. Create notebooks by topic: Survival skills, forage food, stealing cable - you can take meeting notes and send them to the far corners of the world.

All this leads me to this conclusion: whatever technology you have in your back pocket, it must work for you and your purposes. Otherwise it gets dusty on your digital shelf. Who needs that? Ask yourself: what are you trying to do? What problem are you trying to solve? What ideas are you trying to capture or investigate? Mostly, who are you trying to connect with - why have all this technology if you aren't connecting on one level or another to someone else? Humans need other humans. The expansion of thoughts and ideas is what helps us evolve and generally makes us smarter.

Be it trying to run from the zombie army, or trying your hand at amateur photography - the point is try, experiment, play and have fun.

To quote the wise Dr Suess: *"If you never did, you should. These things are fun and fun is good!"*

Thank you!

A heartfelt thank you for reading this far, for buying or downloading this book, and for taking the time to show interest in the work that we, the contributors within the book, do.

If I may return to my first entry in the book ... now it's your turn to reflect on your own emergency rations, your own *#EdTechRations*. Are you more of, as Teresa MacKinnon says in her review, a pragmatist who admits to relying on sensible shoes and stationery, a competitive type with their heart monitor and cycling accessories, a fashion victim, a style guru, a lover, a maker, an artist or poet ... ?

Whichever style or author you most relate to or find synergy with, write about your *#EdTechRations* and share it. Blog it, tweet, it, FaceBook it, sketch it, film it. But whatever you do, after reaching this stage in the book, don't just ignore it.

About David Hopkins

Before becoming a Learning Technologist in 2007 I progressed through a couple of 'careers'. After graduating from Kingston University my degree in Geology served me well for a few years in the UK oil & gas industry, based in Reading then London. From an interest in the growing world of internet start-ups and the boom of the dot-com era I retrained myself in the fields of internet development and communications. Being on the south coast of England meant I was in an area of creativity, and quickly found my niche. It wasn't until I joined the Business School at Bournemouth University that I began to learn about learning, about being a Learning Technologist, and supporting distance learning students and a fully-online degree. It was here I developed my understanding of learning technology, and the fact that I realised there was so much I didn't know. I started my journey to find out 'what is a Learning Technologist?'

What is, at the time of writing, very nearly exactly ten years later, and now at Warwick Business School, I am still asking the same questions, finding familiar difficulties in different systems, different tools, different teams and different cultures. Not everything is the same, but much of the issues I've faced, and others around me too, are still here and still being addressed. Much of the technology on my desk or in my pocket is radically different and markedly more powerful than when I started this journey, but we still seem to be searching for answers on how we use it 'appropriately' and in a 'considered' manner to enhance, not detract, from the purpose of its intent– namely, for learning.

This, my fourth book, is a culmination of my work and those I learn from and respect from within my personal learning network (PLN). Ideas are shared, help is offered, guidance is accepted, and collaborations are welcomed in such a way that I don't think any other 'business' could comprehend – can you see any other businesses allowing their staff to share their work, their 'secrets' like we do. Openess only goes so far to describing how we work and think. We are 'open' with both our work as well as our ideas, and this goes far beyond the research or investigative side of what we do. We're 'open' with our attitudes too. Perhaps this is what to be 'open' is really about?

Books

Other books by David Hopkins - *http://bit.ly/EdTechBooks*

- 2013 QR Codes in Education. *http://bit.ly/QRCodesBook*

- 2013 What is a Learning Technologist? *http://bit.ly/whatisLT*

- 2015 The Really Useful #EdTechBook. *http://bit.ly/EdTechBook*

- 2017 Emergency Rations. #EdTechRations. *http://bit.ly/EdTechRations*

49512991R00077

Made in the USA
San Bernardino, CA
26 May 2017